#SOBLESSED:

The Annoying Actor Friend's Guide to Werking in Show Business

By @Actor_Friend

D1365437

For –

all of the true Annoying Actor Friends out there, who continue to live life, blissfully unaware that they are complete and utter douche-bags.

I am forever #grateful. Eternally #blessed.

TABLE OF CONTENTS

Introduction

INTRODUCTION

EQUITY MEETING

Oh, hey first rehearsal as a company member, AEA, aaaaaaaand chorus deputy! Ayeeeeee!

*

Welcome to the first day of school! You hold in your hand *the* essential how-to-succeed-in-show-business manual that will, with out a doubt, teach you how to #werk. This book is a spin-off of the Twitter account, AnnoyingActorFriend (@Actor_Friend), which was created to spread awareness of annoying actor behavior on social media websites. As time went on, the account took on other subjects like the *Rebecca* scandal, Russell Crowe in *Les Miserables*, and eventually a fully-realized blog recapping episodes of season two of *Smash*, called *SMASH Don't Give a Shit!*

I'm totes excited to break free of the chains that

bound me to 140 characters, but first I want to lay out a few ideas to keep in mind as you commit this book to memory…

1.) This book is the shit. It should be your bible as you navigate this business.

2.) If something written within seems a bit unrealistic, know that it probably happened to someone.

4.) If something sounds a bit too familiar, it probably happened to you.

5.) If there is a social media statement that feels oddly like something said by someone you know, or possibly yourself – it most likely was.

6.) The statements in ***bold italics*** that follow each chapter title are 100% real and were found on Twitter.

7.) Learn the following terms and decide which one you relate to more…

AWARESIE *(n.)***:** Intelligent followers of @Actor_Friend who are aware of the negative implications of social media masturbation.

UNAWARESIE *(n.)***:** The antithesis of an Awaresie. The Unawaresie is known to use social media as a platform to spread awareness of their #blessedness. They use hashtags without being ironic.

8.) Study the differences between these two words…

WERK *(v.)***:** The art of making shit happen in one's

career and kicking ass while doing it. Werking is fun. It encompasses performance, networking, and all-around awesomeness.

WORK *(v.):* The physical and mental effort performed to achieve a goal. Working is hard. Sometimes shit takes work and not #werk. There is a difference between the two and their individual usage in this book is deliberate.

9.) Tell everyone you know to buy this book. #ShamelessSelfPromotion

Finally, I would be remiss if I did not acknowledge the precise moment that triggered the birth of Annoying Actor Friend. On a hot day in July of 2012, a friend of mine sent me a screen capture of a status update written by their actor friend. It read:

When it rains, it pours! Grateful beyond belief, and overwhelmed in the best way by all the good things happening... Hey Universe, you rock, but I cannot catch ALL of these giant raindrops myself... Can I share some with friends who need it right now so we can all play in the rain?? :)

Seven minutes later, Annoying Actor Friend was born. I want to sincerely thank the actor out there that invited us all to play in their rain. Without them, and people like them, none of this would have been possible.

***

1 ARE YOU #BLESSED?

I'm so blessed to be able to utilize the opportunity to live and create as an actor. No matter where this road goes I'm enjoying the ride.

*

Before you can learn to #werk in show business, you must ask yourself: "Are you #blessed?" Being #blessed is not something that comes quietly. You aren't born with it. It is thrust upon you with little warning. One day you're content with the prospects of being a doctor and then – BAM! – You're like, "I gotta dance." It's a calling. Just like when the nuns in *Sister Act* asked Deloris Van Cartier when she got "the call" to join the sisterhood, actors receive a special call from the spiritual god of theatre that tells us to go forth and spread our gift.

Receiving "the call" is the precise moment when an actor becomes #blessed. It's when they first discover they are destined to #werk. However, thousands of actors get the call to #werk, but that doesn't always mean they will *work*. To be successful in show business, you can't just be #blessed. You have to be #SOBLESSED. The #SOBLESSED actor has an enviable career, and carries with them an ultimate understanding of how the industry #werks. Remember, it's no coincidence that the words "Show Business" have the same initials as #SOBLESSED. When we're through, you'll have all the tools needed to truly fulfill your calling.

If you aren't quite sure if you're #blessed, or if you're ever going to be #blessed, here are a few examples of when ordinary people discovered they were #blessed...

"@emmaxpace: When I was 3 I saw Cats and ask my dad if that was a movie and he told me "no, those are actual people performing""

"@drewchandler: Opening night, age 11. I perspired while I boxstepped & a drop of melted Ben Nye slid on my lips. It was the taste of #blessed"

"@baileyford2016: On my 6th birthday when I cried realizing I wasn't Dakota Fanning yet"

The anointing can come from being emotionally affected by a performance, while performing on stage, or even from a deeply-rooted guttural envy you have of someone else's #SOBLESSEDness. It doesn't matter how you become #blessed. It only matters that it happens. Once you are #blessed, you are ready to embark on a journey that will take you deep into the mythical kingdom of Manhattan, and all its surrounding wonder. This book will serve as a guide in your quest to find the true meaning of being #blessed, and by the end you will be #SOBLESSED.

If you said, "yes" to being #blessed, then consider it the "places call" – for your destiny.

2 WHAT DO YOU DO WITH A BFA IN THEATRE?

Done with all of my college auditions :) I'm so satisfied with myself! Now all I need to do is sit back relax and wait for acceptance #yayme

*

The majority of children are raised with the idea that college comes after high school, and those children are also raised to believe that a college degree will one day be mandatory if they want to get a good job and be successful within their chosen field. To that, I say, "LOL," and to the first person who decided to create a major dedicated to the craft responsible for jazz hands and coffee grinders, I hope you are sleeping tight within your blankets woven out of hundred dollar bills.

Assholery isn't taught. You're born with it. Now, it's time to find an establishment that will cultivate it into a career. Before we proceed down the dreaded path of

5

college applications and the countless different versions of one audition you are going to have to prepare, I want you to decide if pursuing a degree in theatre is the first step you want to make in your quest to be #SOBLESSED. If you're deciding to blow off keggers and eight a.m. ballet class to move right to the Boulevard of Broken Dreams, I suggest you skip to the next chapter, *Pounding the Pavement*. If you're a high school student seriously considering applying in the near future, or you're just as bizarrely fascinated with clinging to your youth as I am, then you may continue reading.

Some of you might still be in college, some of you might be years away from college, and if you're like me, you graduated college about twenty-five minutes ago. Many elements of pursuing a BFA in theatre (musical and straight acting) have not changed since the dark ages before The Common App, when each application had to be filled out manually, and I had to write my Social Security Number down countless times. In fact, perhaps the most useful skill I ever learned in the entire BFA process was the accidental memorization of my own Social Security Number. It was pretty much downhill after that.

Certain things have not changed. You still need to pay an application fee AND an audition fee, each school wants a different version of the same audition, and the major itself has only further evolved into a degree in Commercial Theatre that will box you up into the most marketable version of you possible – which may include, but is not limited to, whichever successful graduating senior that you most closely resemble from the last few years.

The best place to begin gathering information about various BFA programs is over at CollegeConfidential.com. That is where we will begin our journey. So, pour yourself a stiff drink and let me regale you with tales from the seedy underbelly that is auditioning for a degree in theatre…

WHAT YOU'LL LEARN AT COLLEGECONFIDENTIAL.COM

The funny thing about College Confidential is that it's really not at all confidential. Some mom will go on there to ask a question about the school and then a freshman named fansie24601 will respond and then another freshman named bitch0FLivin will be like, "OMG! I'm a freshman, too! It's me, Cadence! Who is this?" Then fansie24601 will immediately follow up with, "Hey Cadence! It's Braxton!" And that's around the time the "confidential" part gets thrown under the bus as Cadence and Braxton gush about their school for posts upon pages just in case their dean chooses to patrol the forum.

Furthermore, even when you're trying to stay "confidential" on College Confidential, someone's parent will undoubtedly out you. I found an old post of mine (because OK fine this wasn't my first trip to the message board of musical madness), and sure enough, one of my classmate's parents had completely exposed my identity. Keep your parents at a bandwidth-distance of 56kbit/s (that's dialup) at all times. They will find a way to ruin your life in the most endearing way possible. While we're on the subject, let's take a minute to address what should be your biggest concern right now...

Your Parents

Perhaps the most hashtag-horrifying thing about applying for college is finding out that your parents are more Internet savvy than you thought. That doesn't make them any less awkward. Current parents of prospective freshmen are late Baby Boomers and early Gen X-ers. They use capital letters, punctuation marks, and complete sentences when posting on message boards. It's so retro. Sometimes they attempt to embrace their Millennial child's Twitterhand by shortening a few words to sound more hip. Primarily the words, "daughter" and "son." They simply type D or S. Actually, those are the only two words that ever get the shorthand treatment. Everything else is relatively drawn out and detailed. Example: "My D and I took a lovely trip across the great country of the United States of America to visit the luxurious campus at New York University. My D thoroughly enjoyed their production of *Precious: based on the novel Push by Sapphire: a new musical fable.*"

You are about to embark on a journey that will involve several long distance travel days with your parents. Before you fully commit to this, I want you to perform a critical analysis of your parent or guardian and ask yourself the following questions:

What kind of parent are they?

How will they behave in the waiting area at an audition?

Will they help or hinder my chances?

What sort of mundane questions will they ask during a Q & A?

Will they embarrass me more than usual?

Will they flat out forget about my college visit?

These are all valid concerns and should be taken seriously. Most parents in the waiting area at your auditions will be some sick hybrid of cast rejects from *The Real Housewives* and *Dance Moms*. Don't let them be *your* parents. You don't want to be the kid that didn't get into your top choice because you mom wouldn't stop bragging to the student monitor about your performance in the eighth grade production of *Sweeney Todd*. Contrariwise, you don't want parents who are so disconnected that you miss an audition because your dad thought it was, "next weekend."

If you can pinpoint what kind of parent you're dealing with before this entire shit show of an audition season starts, then you will definitely have a #legup! The ideal parent is the one that follows your lead and stands in the back quietly. Strike that – the ideal parent is the one that just gives you their Amex and says, "Let me know how it works out!"

College Audition Coaches

When I was auditioning for school, my audition

coach was a mirror and an audio recorder. I had no idea there were hundreds of theatrical professionals out there making tens of dollars coaching high school students how to win a lottery. Thanks a lot, Mom! Had I known, maybe I would have brought a repertoire book, styled wardrobe, and slick demeanor to my auditions instead of the vocal selections from *Side Show*, a wink, and a prayer.

The two most popular go-to's for college audition coaching are Musical Theatre College Auditions (MTCA) and Mary Anna Dennard (MOO). MTCA was founded by Ellen Lettrich and boasts a boatload of coaches you may or may not recognize, and Mary Anna Dennard runs her business rogue because her nickname is MOO and I have yet to find out why. The obvious cow connotations came to mind but a simple Google image search will inform you that she is not at all overweight and happens to be a MILF (Musically Informed Lovely Female).

MTCA employs over thirty talented and successful performers whose passion is coaching the next crop of hopefuls that will eventually rise up and take their mentors' future jobs. You see, everything exists together in a delicate balance. As a Broadway performer, we need to understand to respect all the creatures, from the high school fan to the non-equity. When we get older, our careers become the grass, and the youth eat the grass. And so we are all connected in the great Circle of Life.

Mary Anna Dennard (MOO) is from Dallas, Texas and has so many close connections with several different theatre schools that she actually hosts her own unified auditions for her students. Of the fourteen schools that attend her MOO-nifieds (I swear to God, I did not make that shit up. That's actually what they call it), only a handful of them come from states that do not smoke ribs, pulled pork, or brisket at the Big Apple Barbecue in Madison Square Park every June. I mean, these are some t-bone-tastic schools, and while I'll get to Texas State University's inevitable Karen-Cartwright-rise-to-conservatory-crown-jewel-status in a moment, the states represented at the MOO-nifieds are giving me a better idea as to why Mary Anna Dennard is nicknamed MOO (because she's literally surrounded by cattle!).

Do I recommend an audition coach? I'm not going to tell you what to do with your parents' money. Kids have been getting into college without a coach for years. But like, I want you to consider one thing – just how much of a #hotmess are you? Do you audition with *Wicked*? #hotmess. Is your headshot your senior portrait? #hotmess. Do you think the word "slate" is just the name of an online magazine dedicated to politics, technology, business, and the arts? #hotmess.

I was such a #hotmess, I didn't even know Carnegie Mellon had a reputable program until like my second semester of college. How could I have noticed wallflower CMU when Michigan was YouTube seducing me with *Edges* and *The Battery's Down*? That's why it's extremely important to research every option available. Now, I know what you're thinking...

There. Are. So. Many. Schools!!!

There are over fifty-five separate MT programs with their own forum on College Confidential and I think there are around forty-seven different acting studios at NYU alone. Before you start deciding which school to apply to, make a choice between majoring in musical theatre or what people call "straight acting," where you only do "straight plays." Straight acting majors are referred to as such because the gay/straight ratio in a straight play's cast typically tends to tip unusually straight. Find the major that #werks for you and choose wisely!

Needless to say, senior year of high school for a kid who wants to sing, dance, and act blows, and that's really saying something considering you've already completed three years of high school being the kid who wants to sing, dance, and act. While all your friends are simply sending out essays, applications, and test scores, you're doing all of that plus flying to exotic cities like Pittsburgh, Cincinnati, and San Marcos, Texas to present roughly six minutes of material in the hopes of gaining admittance into an establishment that will provide you with the training you need to reach the impossible dream of becoming a serious actor on the Great White Way, in *Sesame Street Live*, or at Ellen's Stardust Diner. In addition to all of this stress weighing heavily on your shoulders, you're missing the Winter Formal!

I hope you don't get too concerned with which school might be the right one for you. Instead, I suggest looking through a stack of Playbills to see where everyone got their education and apply to the ten or twelve that pop up the most. Or, if you happen to be making a choir trip to NYC, stalk your favorite performers at the stage door and personally ask them where you should go to school – because they may think where they went was shit. Also, research the top casting directors and see where they went and go there, too. Actually, if you want to be really ahead of everyone else your age, you should research where the current casting *interns* went to school.

For purposes of this book, each school discussed will be broken up into its own section and put to task with the same questions. Here is a breakdown of how I will analyze each of the separate BFA programs...

[INSERT THEATRE SCHOOL]

What is [Theatre School]'s Nickname?

Some programs have a nickname that is popular to use and I will also include other nicknames for the school that I've heard. I swear I did not come up with the lesser-known nicknames. #honest. #winkyface.

How Smart Do I Have to Be to Attend [Theatre School]?

Schools will consider your GPA and the following standardized tests: SAT, SAT II, ACT, and SAT III: The Legend of Curly's Gold. The mere mention of standardized tests is such a friendly reminder to me that there were responsibilities during my teenage years outside the International Thespian Society and finding a way to talk myself into a varsity letterman jacket for *Bye Bye Birdie*.

My first introduction to the intimidating evaluation process invented to judge how good one is at taking tests, known as the SAT (Scholastic Assessment Test), came during a rerun of a show that people who were born before 1990 actually used to watch live. That show was *Saved by the Bell*. In one particular episode, Bayside High junior, Zack Morris, and his five friends received their SAT scores. This was back in the archaic days when the SAT was graded up to 1600 instead of the current 2400. The original *Saved by the Bell* class scored in the following order of highest to lowest: Zack – 1502, Screech – 1220, Jessie – 1205, Lisa – 1140, Kelly – 1100, and Slater – 1050.

I'm not going to confuse you with crazy words like "25th percentile" and "Phi Beta Kappa," because I'm too lazy to Google "percentile," and the only thing I know about "Phi Beta Kappa" involves Mrs. Phi-Beta-Kappa-Peterson. Instead, I am going to rank the SAT qualifications for each school on a scale of Slater to Zack.

How Many Weeks on Broadway Will My Education from [Theatre School] Cost?

Until September 29th, 2014, the Production Contract minimum will be $1,807. I'd like to put into perspective how many weeks an actor will have to work under a Production Contract *minimum* to pay back four years of education at each school. In an effort to omit the obvious grey areas, this estimate will not deduct 10% agent fees, 2% union dues, and 80% for taxes. The number of weeks noted will be based on the theory you banked the entire $1,807 and funneled it right back to your alma mater, instead of to your living expenses and day drinking. So… it might be safe to triple the number of weeks listed that you'll need to work – and just so you know, I mean "work" with an "O." It will not be WERK. Working off your student loans will be ball-busting-bloody-sweaty-guilt-like-when-you-wake-up-next-to-someone-and-think-whatthefuck-did-I-do-with-my-life WORK. #YAYBROADWAY!

What Did You Learn About [Theatre School]?

I have not visited all of these schools. I can't even remember which ones I auditioned for when I was applying for college. I'm not even sure if I have a friend from each school that I researched. Actually, I know that's true because my friends are pretty much made up from a Michigan/CCM/CMU ratio of 50/30/20. For me to get a good feel for what each program has to offer, I spent countless minutes on each school's website. This was exciting, because in some cases I was given a truly unbiased first impression! I will make sure to share with you what I have learned about each school through the rumor mill and from the story they told me on their website. I'll give you a preview: Every school loves them some #angstybeltface and I've yet to find one that hasn't chosen to showcase pictures from their production of *Musical Where the Girls Wear Prairie Boots*.

What is the Audition Process at [Theatre School] Like?

Some schools have so many students clamoring for admission that they actually need to prescreen everyone before granting an official audition. This isn't the type of prescreen some of us are used to now. (The one where some casting associate's second assistant gets to feel super cool for the afternoon.) This particular prescreen requires the student to video tape themselves singing, acting, and #gasp: DANCING.

Once you are granted a coveted LIVE audition, the real shit show starts. Unifieds! Campus visits! Other kids' parents! In this section, I will breakdown what I have learned about each school's particular audition process. If they have a prescreen, I will note it. If there is an ethically questionable "how-to audition" pamphlet, you're going to hear about it. If a school grants you a callback by leading you through secret Wonderland-esque doors, or cuts you by launching you down the Veruca Salt "bad egg" garbage shoot thingy, I'll let you know!

What Are My Odds of Getting Into [Theatre School]?

Anywhere from seven hundred to like a billion eager high school students audition for theatre school every year, but it appears that the average accepted class size in any given program is around twenty-five. That's a lot of tears and broken dreams. Thank goodness there's always AMDA!

In this section, I will also explain what kind of performer for which I think each school is looking. This is a highly educated opinion that I am confident talking about because I know nobody else in the world has the free time in their life to scour YouTube for freshmen showcases. I only #werk 24 hours a week and that leaves me 144 hours to work.

Who Are the Notable Alumni from [Theatre School]?

Every school has at least one and if you think I'm just going to casually list their names then you know nothing about me.

THE SCHOOLS!!!

I have chosen six schools whose programs will be dissected and ranked in no particular order: Carnegie Mellon University, Cincinnati College-Conservatory of Music, Boston Conservatory, New York University, Texas State University, and University of Michigan.

CARNEGIE MELLON UNIVERSITY: SCHOOL OF DRAMA

What is Carnegie Mellon's Nickname?

CMU: Our Students Don't Know What An EPA Is.

How Smart Do I Have to Be to Attend CMU?

Screech at the very least. If you rock your audition, I'm sure they'd take you if you're a Slater. But like, you really have to rock that audition and not just wear cut off sleeves.

How Many Weeks on Broadway Will My Education from CMU Cost?

132 weeks. That's about 2.5 years in *Mamma Mia* or 132 productions of *Glory Days*.

What Did You Learn About CMU?

These bitches love multi-tiered cubes in their set designs and real grass and plants on stage. They also feature two separate downloadable PDFs entitled "Five Facts About the Acting Program" and "Five Facts About the Music Theatre Program." I found these very helpful because they really pinpointed the differences between both programs. For example, the acting brochure was orange and the music theatre one was purple. According to the brochure, that is the only difference between the two programs, so I guess I'd go with orange.

The undergraduate acting/music theatre page is broken down into four main sections. "What You Will Learn" describes each of your four years by using the word "rigorous" more than once, along with, "discipline," "foundation," "sophisticated," "verbally-complex," and "student-directed" (#eek!). "What Opportunities Await" explains the senior showcase and a theatre festival but doesn't really go into detail about hangovers, herpes, or the walk of shame. "What You Will Become" is one of two pages that pimps out CMU's prestigious graduates. This one leads with naming alumni Ted Danson, because everybody in the high school graduating class of 2013 was OBSESSED with *Cheers*. Finally, we have "Who You'll Work With," which lists the faculty. The only name you'll need to memorize is theatre department head, Barbara Mackenzie-Wood (BMW). If you don't get passed all the way to BMW at your audition you might as well just give up on life.

What is the Audition Process at CMU Like?

CMU is the school that brought us no less than two leading actors on *Smash*, so they aren't going to dick around at your audition. They run that shit like a well oiled machine. They could want nothing to do with you, but you'd never know it because the entire process is truly a pleasant experience.

According to the website, students applying to the acting program must prepare one contemporary monologue and one from before 1900. They should each be one minute long and it is clearly stated that you must have read the entire play so you know what the fuck you're talking about. The music theatre major auditions have the same requirements as the acting, but with the addition of two contrasting songs of thirty-two bars each. CMU doesn't suggest reading the libretto to whatever musical your songs are from and it's a good thing. A hundred girls are going to sing "Wanting" from *Rags*, but does anybody really know what that show is about?

CMU recently eliminated their dance audition portion, so all you petrified straight boys who just bought your "my-first-dance-belt" at the local Capezio can relax and let your testicles ease back down from within your abdomen. I believe CMU needed to ditch the dance auditions to make time for all the mysterious rooms you need to pass through before making it to the elusive Barbara Mackenzie-Wood.

CMU auditions sound like you have to jump through more hoops than the *Pippin* revival. They are like the final act of *Harry Potter and the Sorcerer's Stone*. Your vocal audition is the devil's snare, your acting audition is the chess game, and if you make it through all of that alive, you get to do it again for Professor Volde-Wood. (I'm by no means equating Ms. Mackenzie-Wood to Voldemort. This is just an extremely elaborate and forced analogy.)

The difference between Voldemort and the final stage in the CMU audition process is that He-Who-Must-Not-Be-Named was only trying to torture and kill Harry. CMU makes you do *improv*. If they are interested in your talent, you may be asked to perform additional improvisational exercises like jumping around and screaming like a monkey. They may also suggest you run around the room yelling at the top of your lungs. Embrace it! It's art! It's acting! It's raw! But, should you gain admittance to CMU, you may want to make sure you're clear headed in every acting class in the event they pull that shit again. I imagine this is the type of school that would ask you to pretend there were spiders crawling out of your vagina. If you're considering that late-night pot brownie, just say, "no." Unless you like the idea of urinating yourself out of sheer horror in class the next day.

What Are My Odds of Getting Into CMU?

Several answers come to mind and they involve the words: fat, snowball, chance, hell. The class size is around twelve students for each program out of a pool of probably over a thousand applicants.

Who Are the Notable Alumni from CMU?

Two of the strippers from *Magic Mike*, the farmer from *Babe*, Ivy Lynn and Tom Levitt, Angela from *Who's the Boss?*, the guy who sang "Love is On the Way" in *The First Wives Club* movie, the guy who played a gay guy in the first season of *American Horror Story* but not in the second one, Kathleen Marshall's brother, the female Leading Player in *Pippin*, and at least two actors from the original cast of *The Book of Mormon* who are now making workshop royalties off of four companies. #werk.

UNIVERISITY OF CINCINNATI: COLLEGE-CONSERVATORY OF MUSIC

What is the Cincinnati College-Conservatory of Music's Nickname?

CCM: Prairie Hotties.

How Smart Do I Have to Be to Attend CCM?

Kelly Kapowski. A solid Lisa Turtle could get you an academic scholarship.

How Many Weeks on Broadway Will My Education from CCM Cost?

60 weeks in-state and 93 weeks out-of-state. So, "in-state" is like when your show closes after the original star's contract ends, and out-of-state would be like if the producers brought in Tony Danza to keep it alive for another six months.

What Did You Learn About CCM?

The highlight of the musical theatre section of the CCM website is a video of the 2013 graduating class singing a choral arrangement of Craig Carnelia's "Flight." I don't know a tenor alive who didn't think he had found the Holy Grail of Masturbatory Descants when he first stumbled across this beast of a song. I always thought something was missing whenever I watched my friends in vocal performance class shoot for the moon and land among the sharps, and I think what it was, is sixteen people valiantly failing to do it in harmony.

I didn't spend a lot of time researching the drama side of the CCM program. Part of me thinks I'm not the only one. The drama section of their website prominently features a large photo from some play of a naked student covering his bloody groin area in what appears to be an effort to conceal the aftermath of a recently severed penis. Whatever homage this image is playing to Theon Greyjoy, it's a pretty honest representation of what the college audition process feels like.

What is the Audition Process at CCM Like?

For those who are unaware, CCM issues a helpful and brief manual to prospective students with tips on how to give the best audition possible. These "do's and don'ts" are currently published on the CCM website. However, it appears that some of the more controversial suggestions have been omitted since the days in which I carried their manual around like a bible. And like *The Bible*, the CCM "Do's and Don'ts" evoked feelings of guilt, inferiority, and self-loathing.

There was one particular passage that I remember vividly. CCM does not currently endorse it, because it is no longer present in their pamphlets nor printed on their website. Luckily, neither the Internet nor myself forget, and I was able to locate the passage on the website for Viterbo University ("Borrowed liberally from the Cincinnati Conservatory Audition Guidelines") by Googling the following terms that have been eternally burned into my memory: pass, on, the, double, whoppers, with, cheese…

"DO pay attention to your personal appearance … It may be hard, but take a long, objective look at yourself in a mirror and assess what you see. Decide on your best physical presentation. If you need to lose weight or gain muscle, begin as soon as possible — but please do it safely. Visit the dentist, invest in a new hairstyle, pamper your complexion, learn the fundamentals of make-up, get in shape, start working out or jogging. Exercise your mind. Take a dance class or a yoga class or just get some sleep! Eat well and pass on the double whoppers with cheese. Present yourself as a prospective student who will be fun to teach and highly employable after graduation."

(Viterbo.edu. Web. Retrieved 9.16.13)

Can you picture the kind of emotional turmoil that caused this seemingly well-adjusted teenager? I'm serious! I ate a double whopper with cheese every day for lunch in high school, so you can imagine how devastated I was to read that it was a "no-no." Apparently, nothing tastes as good as Broadway feels.

What Are My Odds of Getting Into CCM?

There was a time when CCM had the reputation for cultivating alumni that appeared mass-produced or lacking any distinguishing characteristics from being manipulated by a device with sharp edges used for cutting cookie dough into a particular shape. That's not really the case anymore. After viewing a few freshman showcase videos, it looks like CCM has the monopoly on hot farmers. Like, if you were a smokin' Laurey or Curly in high school, then hightail it to the CCM auditions STAT – after taking a long, objective look at yourself in the mirror, of course! #BurgerKing.

Who Are the Notable Alumni from CCM?

A Broadway butt-load of graduates that include: the not-Julie-Andrews Mary Poppins, the girl who got to sing "Summertime" in the *Porgy & Bess* revival when we all thought it was going to be Audra, a bunch of people who've done *Mamma Mia*, another guy making more money than I'll ever see in life off of *The Book of Mormon* workshop royalties, everyone else, and possibly your mom.

You might be thinking, "But what about the

original Sketch from *Hairspray*, or the two oldest Newsies, or the non-dancing Anita? Didn't they got to CCM?" Yes, they did – but much like Millie, a few Glindas, and probably all Melchiors, some people don't graduate.

THE BOSTON CONSERVATORY: MUSIC, DANCE, THEATRE

&

NEW YORK UNIVERSITY: TISCH SCHOOL OF THE ARTS

After much research, thought, and prayer, I have decided to discuss Boston Conservatory and NYU at the same time, less I fall victim of telling many of the same jokes twice.

What Are Their Nicknames?

BoCo and Tisch: We Are Still Relevant. Promise.

How Smart Do I Have to Be to Attend BoCo or Tisch?

NYU is looking for a classic Zack and BoCo would like at least a Kelly Kapowski, but will settle for a Slater. BoCo don't give a shit.

How Many Weeks on Broadway Will My Education from BoCo or Tisch Cost?

134 weeks at BoCo and 136 weeks at NYU. If you want to go to either of these schools you're going to have to be content with sitting down at the Majestic,

Ambassador, or August Wilson for the rest of your life.

What Did You Learn About BoCo and Tisch?

The Theatre Division page on the BoCo website features a video about the program that starts with the opening number from their production of *42nd Street* with large text emblazoned across the screen that reads: THEATRE. I challenge you to sit through something that trite and cheesy longer than you were able to watch Two Girls One Cup.

The rest of the BoCo page is broken down into "Your Training," "Your Teachers," "Your Performance Opportunities," and "Your Future." The "Your Future" section chooses to place *Baby, It's You* practically near the top, and then later lists the words "Constantine Maroulis" and "Tony nomination" next to each other. So, basically I learned that if you go to BoCo, anything is possible.

The NYU website was so difficult to understand that I swear one's ability to navigate it successfully is the first step in the admission process. If you're able to get all the information you need, actually apply to the right program, and not end up taking the LSATs by mistake, you are more qualified to attend NYU than me.

The Tisch School of the Arts at NYU has eight different studios. There are six for acting, one for production and design, and one for musical theatre. The New Studio on Broadway used to be CAP21 and CAP21 is the new AMDA. I'm not sure what that makes

AMDA, but I don't think AMDA was anything to begin with (#burn!).

What are the Audition Processes at BoCo and Tisch Like?

For BoCo, you get four minutes to do two contrasting monologues. The website states that one monologue be "post-war" but they don't specify which war (It could be WWII, but what if they mean Vietnam and you want to do something from *The Crucible*?), and one from "classical literature" (Specifically Shakespeare's histories and comedies. They didn't mention the tragedies. I'm not sure if they'll take problem plays or not, so just do a Bottom or Helena speech from *A Midsummer Night's Dream* to be safe and original.).

BoCo also runs a "rigorous dance audition" and gives you four minutes to sing a ballad and an "upbeat." I've never heard an up-tempo referred to as an "upbeat," but I'm using that term from now on because it sounds cooler.

NYU is fancy so they call their audition an "artistic review." They require two contemporary monologues be performed in less than two minutes. The music theatre "artistic review" tacks on two thirty-two bar contrasting songs with (and I am not kidding here) a suggested movement evaluation during one of the songs. There is not a group dance audition in this artistic review. NYU wants you to literally choreograph something yourself:

"We want to see you move! When preparing for your singing evaluation, please add movement to one of the two song selections. It can be specific choreography or free movement -- be inspired! ... The added movement/dance may include elements of (but not limited to) ballet, jazz, modern, African dance, hip-hop, folk dance, tap dance (no tap shoes, please), acrobatics and martial arts. Include anything that demonstrates full body expressiveness and love of movement. Be creative and incorporate any movements that you love to do and look great doing! ... Approach the movement with an open spirit and a sense of play. Bring all of yourself to the dance. Celebrate you!"

(NYU.edu. Web. Retrieved 7.14.13.)

Seriously, NYU? Would holding a proper dance audition put you guys under financially? You're asking kids to break into tap-less time-steps during "Giants in the Sky" or bust out some martial arts in the middle of "Hello, Young Lovers"? As ridiculous as the multitude of awkward images crossing my brain at this very moment may be, and how incredibly lame, lazy, and flat out emotionally scarring it is to put all prospective Tisch music theatre majors through this, I like...kinda wanna see that shit! I think adjudicating an artistic review for the New School on Broadway has just moved to the top of my bucket list. #CelebrateYou.

What Are My Odds of Getting Into BoCo and Tisch?

Back in the days when the cow from the 2002 *Into the Woods* revival was a student, there really was a prestige associated with BoCo. Now, with a desired class size of around sixty, BoCo could be accepting over one hundred students a year to meet that quota. Your odds of getting in are better, but how does that translate to the classroom?

You're going to get strict, solid training at BoCo, but potentially at the cost of being surrounded by two hundred and fifty theatre divas. If you want to trap yourself in a studio with that many non-equity delights, you could just wait until March, and spend a weekend at NETCs. If you're someone who benefits more from individual attention, BoCo might not be the school for you. If my education is costing a quarter of a million dollars, I don't just want good training, I want the faculty doing my effing laundry.

It's a similar situation at NYU. At any given moment, there are over a thousand drama students. I just don't see how it's possible for one establishment to handle that many anger and tears monologues. NYU differs from BoCo in that it will always skew in favor of grades over talent. If you actually read the books assigned in English class instead of skimming sparknotes.com, but you sing on the legal limit of the pitch, you may want to try NYU. If you can kick your face and screlt an E especially well, but you pronounce that word, "expecially," then maybe go for BoCo.

Who Are the Notable Alumni from BoCo and Tisch?

BoCo: Karen Cartwright.

NYU: A shit ton of people who've won Academy Awards, Tonys, and Emmys, and a shit ton of other people who are like, "Ugh. That person? Really? Of *all* the people in our class?"

TEXAS STATE UNIVERSITY: DEPARTMENT OF THEATRE AND DANCE

What is Texas State's Nickname?

Texas State MOO-niversity! – Nobody's calling it that. I just decided to because it's in Texas and they have cows and NOT because half the classes of '16 and '17 attended the MOO-nifieds discussed earlier.

How Smart Do I Have to Be to Attend Texas State?

Slater. Any Slater will do. They'll take the Slater that wanted to date Tori or the one that allegedly requested that Larry in the *A Chorus Line* revival wear sleeves.

How Many Weeks on Broadway Will My Education from Texas State Cost?

This school is so great with scholarships that you might actually get away with one year on a tiered Production Contract tour and a summer at the Goodspeed Opera House.

What Did You Learn About Texas State?

The musical theatre department was taken over by actress Kaitlin Hopkins, in 2009. Since then, the school has featured a faculty primarily of working New York actors who I may not recognize, but for some reason really have their shit together when it comes to developing a solid program. The website, however, is straight out of 1998. I think it was made on GeoCities.

What is the Audition Process at Texas State Like?

WARNING: There is a prescreen! Texas State asks that you submit a video that includes one contemporary monologue, and two contrasting songs no longer than thirty-two bars each. They also suggest that if you have dance experience to add that in at the end – but it isn't required. Um... Why the hell is it NOT required? This is genius. Unlike NYU, where they ask that you incorporate movement into your vocal artistic review, Texas State requests that you present an entirely separate piece dedicated to dance. It can be a one-minute number, or you could just present random dance moves! The exact dance moves listed include, but are not limited to: leaps, jumps, battements and/or turns (I guess you can do those two at the same time if you want), buffalo, Irish, clog, and other technical elements like jazz square and isolations. I suppose the jazz square and isolations means they are auditioning you to be in the graduating class of 1986.

What Are My Odds of Getting Into Texas State?

Since Texas State is considered an up and coming contender that is so affordable, kids have been known to turn down CMU, CCM, and Michigan to attend. It's safe to say that in about ten years, Texas will be the new Michigan. They are all about diversity and making the best unique version of you, so their class sizes are not much more than twelve. The competition is dense because the price point is so low. You may get turned off by the fact it is just some school out in Texas, but I urge you to factor cost chiefly into your college decision making. Remember, you are pursuing a degree in musical theatre. Say it with me, "I am going to pursue a college degree in MUSICAL. THEATRE." #broadway. #tonys. #dreamsbeforelogic.

Who Are the Notable Alumni from Texas State?

All those fresh and earnest assholes you see showing up at auditions around June. Wide-eyed recently graduated theatre majors are the crabgrass of Broadway.

UNIVERSITY OF MICHIGAN: SCHOOL OF MUSIC, THEATRE & DANCE

What is Michigan's Nickname?

Michigan: The New CCM.

How Smart Do I Have to Be to Attend Michigan?

A sensible Screech – or Jessie before she got hopped up on caffeine pills.

How Many Weeks on Broadway Will My Education from Michigan Cost?

57 weeks in-state and 115 weeks out-of-state. I wouldn't sweat it. Your résumé will say, "University of Michigan."

What Did You Learn About Michigan?

Remember that time when all the envious MTs of the world dogged on CCM for being the elite-cookie-cutter-triple-threat-we-hate-you-because-you-go-there-and-we-don't-school? I'm not exactly sure when this program "crossed over" and became the Crown Jewel of BFAs, but I'm guessing it had something to do with YouTube.

Michigan was always a reputable program and there were notable alumni before the dawn of Twerking By The Cakes, but there was something about the way Andrew Keenan-Bolger and Jake Wilson latched onto the Internet's new way of delivering original content that helped set the school apart from everybody else and bring its relevance into the homes of high schoolers everywhere. They were somewhat pioneers in their own way. Michigan's ability to be the first program to find a way to mass-market to the *Wicked* Generation is probably why their students are so successful today and NOT AT ALL because of any alumni who might be involved with casting.

What is the Audition Process at Michigan Like?

PRESCREEN! It's pretty much the same rigmarole as Texas State, except it's articulated on the website better because it's Michigan and they're so perfect I think I'll just kill myself. They require two monologues, two sixteen bar cuts, and WATCH OUT because here comes that solo choreographed dance again! I still want to see the singer-who-moves (and by, "moves" I mean, "can walk") prescreens from these schools. We live in a cynical world, and I am not accusing any of these schools of playfully making fun of a #hotmess prescreen, but if we think they aren't at some point, we're kidding ourselves. I dare you to find me an agent or casting director who hasn't at least once emailed an actor's submitted headshot to their friends because it's too ridiculous not to share. If you can find me someone in this business that is truly professional enough to have treated other people's lives and dreams with respect 100% of their entire career, I will quit the business and become a paleontologist.

If you are truly #blessed enough, you'll receive a live audition appointment that pretty much consists of presenting the same material from your prescreen – with the exception of a group dance class in substitution of the at-home *Flashdance*-esque choreographed requirement. I wish every prospective Michigan student, including the budding Sancho Panzas of the world, gave these mandatory videoed dance requirements a big fat #blowme and just did three minutes of "What a Feeling."

After you attempt to prove you are a triple threat, they throw a piano/sight reading test in there just to fuck with you. #HolyToneDeafProblems! I would have been up-shit-creek at these auditions! The only thing I knew about solfège when I was seventeen was whatever Maria von Trapp taught me. (If you rolled your eyes at that reference it means I'm doing a good job!) The only thing I remember from my college sight-reading/piano classes is something about Charlie Goes Down And Eats Big Fat Cock.

On the drama end of the Michigan spectrum, there is no need for a prescreen. Michigan don't give a shit about acting, so you can just walk right off the street and do two monologues about as easily as a Michigan grad can take their cap and gown off and walk right onto a Broadway stage. You may, however, be asked to participate in a bit of old-fashioned improv. Not so much "Scenes from a Hat," improv and more like "Sing a Folk Song" or "Relate a Childhood Experience" kind of improv. What bad luck must it be for the kid who has to follow some girl's rendition of "This Land is Your Land" with a childhood memory about how they went as a Ninja Turtle for Halloween three years in a row or the time their stepfather touched them? Auditions are hard, y'all.

What Are My Odds of Getting Into Michigan?

The class sizes are around twenty and the faculty is extremely selective. If you are a talented and easily moldable student with limited diversity and personality, you could potentially have a better chance than someone else. I'm not saying that you need to have been manufactured in a laboratory, but it certainly wouldn't hurt your chances!

Who Are the Notable Alumni from Michigan?

Neil Patrick Harris' partner, Kyle Bishop, one of the Fosters, everyone who has probably ever played

Olive or Coneybear in *Spelling Bee*, someone from *Glee*, and the class of 2007.

DO YOU NEED A BFA TO BE #SOBLESSED?

It's all a crapshoot, and while choosing which college to attend is truly one of life's most monumental decisions that will forever dictate your future, it will certainly not be the last one like it. I would not be where I am today if I had chosen a different school, and who's to say I'd be better or worse off than I am now? Who knows? If I got into my first choice, maybe I'd have been knifed on the way to jazz class in the dark alleyways of Cincinnati (or Ann Arbor, Boston, Pittsburgh, etc. – because I'm not telling you where I did or didn't go! #sorrynotsorry). Everything happens for a reason, and if you don't get what you want in life, it's a good idea to go right on thinking that whatever you wanted would have eventually killed you. That is what I tell myself whenever my agent gives me feedback like, "They went another direction."

Make a decision and trust that it's the right one. Go to college for a solid reason, not because you think it's what you're supposed to do. Go to college for a degree. Go to college for training. Go to college to make connections. Don't go to college under the assumption it will automatically get you anywhere in life. Don't go to college under the assumption that a true triple threat still exists. Learn one thing and learn how to do it better than anyone else. Be the best singer or the best actor or the best dancer or the best looking. If you can't be the best at one of those attributes, then be the best networker. That skill could take you further than anything you might learn in a practice room.

3 POUNDING THE PAVEMENT

I just booked a film role AND a voiceover gig from 2 different companies without an audition! Why? Cuz God is my homegirl. #grateful

*

Congratulations! You have either officially graduated from college, completely blew off college, or left college for a job that just finished! You are ready to move to New York City. This is where the fun really begins. You are moving to the greatest city in the world. If you can make it here, you'll make it anywhere – except Los Angeles because those cold bitches are lethal.

MOVING TO NEW YORK CITY

Moving to New York City is expensive. I understand this because I still have a Bank of America credit card bill that is laughing at me uncontrollably. Seriously, don't move here until you have a healthy buffer in your checking account provided by your parents. If your parents can spot your rent for a year or two, that's even better! If you have the kind of parents that just dump your Sallie Mae loans in your lap without so much as a two weeks notice, then I suggest saving those summer stock nickels until you have a minimum of three months of survival readily available on the off chance you don't book jobs as quickly as your friends.

Let's discuss the monthly budget of an average actor in New York City:

Rent: $1,000
MetroCard: $112
Cable and Utilities: $200 - $300
Gym: $80 - $180
Voice Lessons (1 x week): $400 (low end)/$1,600 (Liz Caplan)
Dance Classes (4 x week): $256
Student Loans: $500 - $600
Bar Tab: $1,000
Tanning: $80
Office Depot Supplies for Vision Board: $167
Food: $7

Once you have the appropriate amount of savings in your bank account, or at least up to that limit available on a credit card, you are officially ready to take the leap. Now, where should you move?

New York City is made up of the following five boroughs: Manhattan, Brooklyn, Queens, the Bronx, and Staten Island. Personally, I believe that anything above 116th Street in Manhattan is a sixth borough known as Upstate New York City.

When you first move to The City, it is necessary

that your quality of living arrangements come before anything. You might be fresh faced and beautiful, but nobody is going to give a shit about you at first. You might as well be happy with the home and neighborhood you're living in, because it's the only thing that will comfort you when your career is moving perpendicular to your classmates'. Here is what I know about the various boroughs:

Manhattan: If you love the awesomeness of running into people who ask "how have you been?" when all they really mean is "are you working?" – then Hell's Kitchen is for you!

Brooklyn: I went down there a lot this summer and came to the realization that as awesome as I am, I'll never be cool enough to live there.

Queens: Astoria is a fantastic place to live if you like being late everywhere. The N and Q trains are like the two old guys from *The Muppets*, just sitting in their private box out on Ditmars Boulevard, ridiculing our brave attempt to be performers by never getting us to auditions or half hour on time.

The Bronx: There is a zoo that a cobra escaped from a few years ago.

Staten Island: The ferry is free.

It doesn't matter where you live as long as you genuinely enjoy it and are not, in fact, lying to yourself. Do not overstay your welcome in an atmosphere that makes you miserable. Do not pretend that a fifteen-minute walk to the train is OK because they're "short blocks." As much as you love that trendy coffee shop in Greenpoint or the amazing views of the East River from Astoria Park, I suggest you weigh it all against the consistency of the MTA on a busy audition morning in the dead of April, when it's still winter.

HOW I GOT MY EQUITY CARD

I was born Equity. Not everybody is granted the same fortune in life, so I will briefly explain how you can go about joining the one union within the theatrical world that is most definitely a Bottom. IATSE Local One (the Broadway Stagehand union) is totally a Top and the Associated Musicians of Greater New York (Local 802, because they don't need to be at work until the downbeat at 8:02 p.m.) gets paid to watch, leaving AEA as the Bottom. Obviously AEA is a Bottom... Such a Bottom... But not a Power Bottom. AEA is the needy Bottom who keeps insisting that each time the Broadway League (of producers) Tops, it will be "the last time" – but then ends up texting two days later, "Hey... I'm lonely."

Equity Contract

You can join the union simply by being hired under an Equity Contract. This is the ideal situation if you are #blessed enough to go straight to Broadway. If you receive your Equity Card from a regional theatre, it is more than likely that they will only turn you Equity for the final few weeks, thus requiring you to do the majority of the run as both non-union and the brunt of everyone's jokes. You will be left unemployed, with a $1,100 initiation fee, $400 of which must be paid immediately for you to enjoy any of the privileges of being a union member. But, WERK, you're Equity now!

Four A's

Also known as "sister unions," the "Four A's" include: AEA, SAG-AFTRA, AGMA, and AGVA. If you are a member of one A, you can "buy into" another A, after being a union member for one year. A few of the "Four A's" make you jump through various hoops to join their union. SAG-AFTRA requires you to have worked under a Principal Contract with AEA if you want to join their union, but AEA don't give a shit. They're like, "Did you do background work? Do you have $400? Welcome to Equity!"

Actors' Equity's website lists another "sister union" entitled, Guild of Italian-American Actors (GIAA). I clicked on the link AEA provided and it rerouted me to a website called, "Online Pokies." I fucking kid you not. On July 3rd, 2013, the union that takes 2% of my weekly paycheck, linked me to a porn website. OK, it wasn't really a porn website. It was a site for something called a "pokie machine," which is an Australian version of a slot machine. Either way, I'm not sure what Australian slot machines have to do with Italian actors, unless I'm missing something other than the fact that my dues are being funneled into online gaming or the salary of a truly non-eq web designer.

Equity Membership Candidate Program (EMC)

There is a lot of non-union work out there and most of that non-union work exists within union theatres. Equity houses will hire as many free actors as humanly possible. If you've been hired to save a regional theatre a shit ton of money, why not put those weeks toward your Equity Card? If you enter into the EMC program, AEA will gift you with your card after working fifty weeks in participating theatres within a five-year period. If this sounds like a good fit for you, make sure you keep track of your weeks, because when you accumulate fifty, the next theatre that hires you is obligated to put you under a union contract. Once the theatre finds this out, they will not hesitate to throw your ass under the bus and replace you with a non-equity delight.

When Should I Join Equity?

Choosing when to become a member of Actors' Equity Association is somewhat of a controversial decision among many performers. What if I don't get work? Should I wait until I have more credits? What if I'm not old enough for the roles I'm right for? These are all valid questions to ask yourself before you take the leap, and I could make a pretty solid argument for not taking your card right away. However, I must give full disclosure by admitting that I once signed my name on an "unofficial list" at the Equity Building, and was subjected to being a non-equity polyp within the Ursula's Grotto waiting area before being #blessed enough to have my Starbucks confiscated from me upon entering the Equity Lounge to sing eight bars in a studio next to restrooms labeled "Guys" and "Dolls." It's not a happy memory. I don't wish it on anyone. Get your Equity Card as soon as possible. If you still have questions and doubts about whether or not you did it too soon, just ask yourself the following question: "Seriously?"

HOW TO LAND AN AGENT

There is no right or wrong way to land an agent, but the best option is probably by #nailingit at your senior showcase and having someone sign you on the spot. If that doesn't happen, you may have to put in a little extra effort. This shouldn't be too hard, provided you are either twenty-two or hot. It's better if you're both.

Usually you can get your foot in the door of an agent's office just by having someone recommend you. Call all of your friends, ask who represents them, and compile a list. Then ask your friends if they are happy with their representation, and when the majority of them carry off on a diatribe explaining how their agent is the reason they don't get any work, proceed to cross every option off your list.

So, what do you do when there are like a hundred agents and you don't know anything about them or if they'll be able to get you any work? Lucky for you, I've developed a formula for efficiently finding the best agent for you.

Annoying Actor Friend's Agent Algorithms Method

STEP 1.) Gather a bunch of Playbills and read all of the cast bios.

STEP 2.) Make a spreadsheet that lists the actors on the top line and the directors, choreographers, and casting directors they've worked with underneath.

STEP 3.) Google each actor's name to find out who represents them.

STEP 4.) Sort the actors and the people they've worked with into their respective agencies.

STEP 5.) Score the agencies by applying the Annoying Actor Friend Agent Point System.

Actors = 1 point.
Directors = 2 points.
Choreographers = 3 points.
Casting Offices = 5 points.

STEP 6.) You should now have a healthy list of agents that are ranked from highest to lowest, based on how often their clients work, how big their casting footprint is, and how much they can do for your career.

Easy right? There's always a way to cheat the system! Success is never random. It's calculated.

The *Annoying Actor Friend's Agent Algorithms Method* gives you an idea of how much clout an agent has before meeting with them. Remember, you are interviewing them as much as they are interviewing you. It's imperative to make sure you know a sixth or seventh choice before you walk in the door.

Getting the Meeting

Now that you have a list of agents who would be #grateful to have you on their roster, add a few "safety agents" to submit to just in case. I suggest finding about a hundred. Most agents accept submissions via email, but I am sure none of them would kick you out of bed for sending a retro hardcopy headshot they can promptly toss in the trash after making a few jokes about your credits and the composition of your photo. It's probably safest to submit both ways.

Hardcopy submissions might be dated, but at least you know where you stand with them. Although the process of using headshots, labels, envelopes, and stamps could potentially bankrupt you, at least you'll know your submission is obligated by the government to reach its destination. Email submissions can always find an excuse to get lost in cyberspace or the agent's spam folder. While the convenience and quickness of it all can be alluring, you never know where your impulses are going to go after hours behind a computer screen zombie-fies you. One time I got so stressed-out while putting together submissions, that when I was done I self-medicated with a little Vicodin left over from an old audition injury. I awoke the next morning to find I had emailed a casting director to tell them how awesome I was, and apparently tried to see how hard I could bite my hand without feeling anything. I was left with an unsightly scar and the casting director never responded. I'll let you guess which scar lasted longer.

When putting together an agent submission, the necessity to draft the perfect cover letter will hinge on how far along you are in your Actor Life Timeline. If you're a little older, but have reasonable credits, a simple and clear cover letter should suffice. If you are inexperienced, you might need to work a little harder to construct an eye-popping cover letter to grab attention. If you are fresh out of college and really attractive, your cover letter can be a literal transcription of the Swedish Chef's popcorn scene from *The Muppets Take Manhattan*, and no less than 85% of the agents you submit to are guaranteed to call you in for a meeting.

Once you have finished the submission process, sit back and wait for the meetings to pile up. Since you are reading this book, I have no doubt in my mind that a shit-ton of agents will be contacting you. If more than one agent offers you a contract, pick the one that scored highest on the *Annoying Actor Friend's Agent Algorithms Method*. It doesn't matter if you click better with a different agent. You're not there to make friends. You're there to make your dreams come true.

HOW TO PISS OFF YOUR AGENT

Sometimes agents need a little help doing their job. I'll bet you've often heard about auditions happening that you were right for and thought, "Why wasn't I submitted for that?" In the dark ages, before smartphones, Kickstarters, and Lea Michele being a celebrity, people used to pass around PDFs of things called "The Breakdowns." If you were on one of those elite lists, you were considered secret royalty. The Breakdowns told you everything you needed to know about what projects were currently auditioning around town. If friends got wind that you had access to The Breakdowns, they'd hound you until you created your own special list with them on it. This concept of The Breakdowns is completely moot now, and I would worry I'm dating myself by mentioning it at all – except joke's on you, this all happened when I was up for one of the kids in Jason Robert Brown's *13*.

Having access to The Breakdowns was great because you could hold your agent accountable for being a douche-bag. If you saw something you thought you were right for, it was easy to nag your agent about it, on the off chance they completely looked you over. I think an agent's favorite question to hear from an actor is probably, "Did you push for this?" Having your finger on the pulse of opportunity is going to make or break your career when you're first starting out.

Things were simpler when The Breakdowns were floating around. Now, to find out what projects you're not being submitted for, you have to hack into BreakdownsExpress.com. Didn't your BFA program offer computer nerd seminars during your career prep class? Oh – Well, I'm not going to tell you how to gain access to BreakdownsExpress.com because I'd be relinquishing my power to you and I have no clue if we're the same type. Consider it a favor. When you do figure out how to get onto BreakdownsExpress.com, you'll also find out whom your agent is submitting alongside or in lieu of you. Just when you think your agent has finally figured out what you're best for, they'll toss in someone with you whom you find to be completely untalented and wrong for the part, thus leading you to believe your agent hasn't a fuck of a clue what is up.

As you get more famous, the need to police your agent will lessen. Eventually, you'll start getting seen for more roles based on how well you perform at auditions and at Mark Fisher Fitness. Until then, put in the extra legwork to make certain you're not the third backup client on your agent's roster. Few things in life are more embarrassing than showing up to an audition studio for a voice lesson and seeing a list on the monitor of all the auditions you weren't invited to. You could venture to say that maybe you were submitted and casting passed on you – but if you're following this handbook correctly, you've attended the same bars and colleges as the people in charge, so you should be getting called in for everything.

THE STUDIOS

You're going to be pounding that pavement and #werking those feet all over New York City, so you better have a good pair of walking shoes – and I'm not suggesting LaDucas because they've been known to fall apart ever since they went non-eq. After a few months, you'll grow numb to the usual suspects you see at every audition, and the studios you attend weekly will begin to feel like second homes to you – but like *August: Osage County* type-homes where you have love/hate relationships with all the dysfunctional family members that never seem to leave.

Every year, a new audition studio pops up. Once you finally find your juju at one location, everybody will start holding their auditions somewhere else. Having been to all of the audition studios, here are few knee-jerk reactions I have when I hear exactly where I need to truck my ass to in an effort to book a job...

Actors' Equity Audition Center

You'll meet a lot of actors who are truly #SOBLESSED, they've never even been inside the Actors' Equity Audition Center. The new studios opened in March of 2013, but I have not even set foot in the Equity Building since the monitor treated my beverage like a cup of grande-half-caff-soy-sarin-gas.

Telsey + Co.

Oh, Telsey... Oh... Telsey, Telsey, Telsey. I think I'll just leave it at that. I don't want to ruin my relationship with Telsey. If this book ever warrants a sequel, I think I'll call it, *#GRATEFUL: Thank You, Telsey.*

New 42nd Street Studios

Windows. Space. Celebrities in the elevator. Celebrities at lunch. A special lanyard to enter the building that *also* gets you a discount at Pax. You have arrived. Unless you're not there for rehearsal. Then you'll just feel like an audience member on a backstage tour – but like an audience member that's pissed off they're on a backstage tour because they should be in the show. If you do find yourself at an audition there, make sure to call it "New 42" as many times as you can. It will give the waiting room residents (and maybe even the casting director!) the impression that you've rehearsed there before. #makingmemories.

Alvin Ailey

I've only auditioned for serious projects at Alvin Ailey. It's *Alvin Ailey*. If you're auditioning at "Ailey," you gotta be going in for true masterpieces like *The Little Mermaid* or *Shrek* – or a guaranteed smash hit like the recent Broadway revival of *Funny Girl*.

The Ford/Hilton/Foxwoods/Whatever They Call It Now

Consider this dismaying observation: This studio has no windows and no clocks, which offers you this chilling challenge… to find a way to get cell phone reception!

Chelsea, Ripley Grier, and Pearl Studios

Chelsea Studios and Ripley Grier used to be the only competitors, but Ripley was always the IT place. It was bigger. It was closer. It was peach. Then Chelsea Studios opened up a new floor and started pulling all the focus. After that, young and pretty Pearl popped up and everybody started going there, even though it was an entire block further from Midtown. Then, like any #trulyblessed actor, Pearl decided it didn't have enough work and opened up another studio across the street. Pearl Studios became like that friend who workshops Broadway shows by day and performs in one at night. Once Pearl threw down the double-douche-dare, Ripley Grier was like, "Fuck you. We ran this town before you were born!" So they opened up an entire floor and a half up on seventeen. Your move, Chelsea... (LOL! J/k – Chelsea's so over.)

Nola Studios

HAHAHAHAHAHAHAHAHAHAHAHAHA HAHAHAHA!

#REASONSYOUDIDNTBOOKIT

I refuse to admit that the fault of a job not booked ever falls on that of the actor. There is always a reason you didn't book it, and many of them are more common than you realize. I have no doubt you'll find a few of the following reasons familiar...

The Casting Office Doesn't Like You

Legendary casting director, Marion Dougherty, told the Miami Harold in 1991 that, "Casting is a game of gut instinct. You feel their talent and potential in the pit of your stomach. It's about guts and luck." I'm sure that's what it feels like on their side of the table, but when luck doesn't play out on our end, the instinct in the pit of my stomach is that they potentially don't feel my talent.

Forging good relationships with casting offices is the single most important thing you can do when you move here – after being under twenty-five. When you're fresh, casting offices approach you with the curiosity of a dog discovering the squeaking mechanism in a chew toy for the first time. They'll be calling you in for all sorts of projects because you're this fascinating new smell they've discovered. You should revel in this moment because it won't be long until they've ripped the squeaker out and you're left collecting stuffing while they've moved on to something shiny.

Relationships with casting offices can be a lot like dating. There's always an awkward first date where they size you up. This is known as a prescreen. It may take several prescreens before they decide you're worthy to sleep with (get seen by the director) or meet their parents (the entire Last Supper table of creatives and producers). Don't get discouraged if you never get to meet the parents. When a casting office refuses to pass you through to the creative team, it could be simply because they don't like you. It's not because you bombed the audition or aren't right for the role. It's casting's insecurity with your awesomeness. There's a speculation that casting may refrain from putting you in front of the creative team because if you're wrong, you could potentially put their credibility on the line and jeopardize their relationship with a director, thus risking future job opportunities for the office. There's something to that theory – but I still believe that if your relationship with a casting office turns sour, it's definitely an, "It's not you. It's me," situation.

They Went Ethnic

You might want to let this slide because it happens a lot less than it should.

The Accompanist Didn't Know How to Play Your Song

Even after you've questionably noted your music, nervously mumbled some directions, and shakily clapped out a tempo, there will still be an accompanist who has no effing clue how to play your Jason Robert Brown song. Seriously, though – whenever I don't get a callback, I usually find a way to blame the accompanist. It doesn't matter if they played my audition flawlessly. It's still their fault.

Take note of which accompanists are solid and which ones gravitate toward turning all of the "up-beats" in your book into power ballads. For every Liberace at Pearl Studios, there's an accompanist who will play your audition wearing a pair of oven mitts.

They Wanted a Name

Whoever said, "There are no small parts, only small actors," was obviously never a swing or a Little Person. Whether you're up for a starring role or a track in the ensemble, the Powers That Be usually have a gravitational pull in their no-no places for actors with attractive credits. If you didn't book a job, it's probably because someone with a prettier résumé came in after you.

It might seem like I'm saying that in order to *get credits* you need to *have credits*, and – yes, that's exactly what I'm saying. #twerk.

They Don't Work Around Show Schedules

Jumping from show to show can be really difficult when one show refuses to work around your other show. The most efficient way to remain gainfully employed is to collect shows like you're storing acorns for the winter. Having a few workshops in your back pocket can ease the sting of a show closing, or the boredom that comes from being employed in a show too long. Most workshops are great about working around show schedules. However, I can't tell you how many TV roles and national commercials I *so* would have booked if they had found a way to work around my schedule.

You Were Too Good Looking

Sometimes you're just too good looking to book a job. It happens. It's your cross to bear. Nine times out of ten, if you miss out on a role, it's because the director didn't want your good looks to distract from the lead. That is why I don't recommend asking your agent for feedback. Being told you're too good looking for a role is demoralizing.

The Reader Skipped Ahead

I've heard about Stone Age days (even way before faxing) when actors had to pick up their sides at their agent's or read the script at the casting office. Talk about #horryifing. Thank god for technology, so you can easily download 8GB of PDFs to your iPad to prepare for a single audition. You might think that carrying a tablet into an audition is doucherific. Well, it ain't nearly as doucherific as learning sixteen different scenes for a role you *might* need to cover, or being told to prepare all of the sides, but pick your favorite – only for the casting director to throw a curve-ball and make you read the one side you studied the least. It's time to go green. I've gotten audition sides for a swing track that easily flattened a square mile of land in the Yucatán. Trees need no longer be slaughtered!

With so many sides for you to prepare, it's inevitable that the reader who has been immersed in the material for days will skip ahead and mess you up. This is called, "When Bad Readers Happen to Good Actors." Should you suffer this horrible fate, you'll at least have someone to blame for not booking the job.

#BOOKEDIT

There is an age-old saying that goes something like, "The average actor has to go on a hundred auditions to book one job." I don't think my agent has ever bothered to find me one hundred auditions. If it took me that long, they'd drop my ass anyway. One hundred auditions is a shit-ton-of-time dedicated to feeling bad about yourself.

If you go on two auditions a week, for about fifty-two weeks, how do you measure a year in the life of an average actor? (The following guesstimate does not include failed callback attempts.)

- $500 in cab fare ($2.50 a ride).
- 4 and 1/16th straight days of non-stop crying (one hour an audition).
- $1,200 in post audition happy hour or comfort fast food.
- 17 bags of Ricolas (4 an audition).
- 25 tablets of Xanax (1/4 a pill per audition).

That's a lot of money to spend on failure. You better make those auditions count! The last thing you want to do is expend all that energy pounding the pavement and end up with your "one booking" being that of a clown in a dinner theatre production of *Hello, Dolly!* Don't let the parade pass you by. That's why I recommend only auditioning for shit that matters. At any given moment, there are twenty shows running on Broadway. That's not even counting the productions waiting in the wings. Between EPAs and ECC singer/dancer calls, you're looking at over a hundred six-month required calls within one-year right there. I challenge you to spend your next one hundred auditions on A-List projects only. If the one out of one hundred theory is true, then you are only ninety-nine auditions away from the appointment that will change your life. Go take on the day. #werk.

4 ON THE ROAD

I refused after college to be a waitress...so once I booked a National Tour out of college I never went back...

*

Congratulations! You've followed my instructions by making the obvious college choice (GO BLUE!) that provided you with a rockin' platform to share your gift and score you some kickass representation (Gersh! Paradigm!), after which, you diligently pounded the pavement until you booked an A-List job. You are about to begin rehearsals for your first Broadway show – oh, what's that? You didn't book a Broadway show yet? It's been like six months. Get your shit together!

Perhaps your Broadway dreams are going to take a little longer to come to fruition. Maybe the Powers That Be don't "see you in the world" of the Broadway company, but think you'd fit in nicely on tour. There's also a chance The Universe wants you to pay a few extra dues in regional theatre. Whatever the reason is, don't freak out. Everyone goes LORT sooner or later. Besides, it might be nice to take a break from The City to see how many Cheesecake Factorys this fine country has to offer! But before you hit the road, it's time to...

TIE UP LOOSE ENDS

Once you've accepted a job out of town, you'll need to learn how to rip yourself out of your comfortable and reliable life routine and potentially share a living space with a person whose behavior you haven't vetted. That's OK because you'll be in a social bubble and required by Equity Law to be besties with your cast no matter what. Knowing that your out-of-town home will be a happy one is given – but what about the one you're leaving behind?

Find an Appropriate Sublet

If you are subletting from someone else, it is perfectly acceptable to just give him or her a few days notice. They won't care because they'll be really excited you got a job! If your name is on the lease, then things will be a bit trickier. First, feel free to immediately post a sublet request on your Facebook wall. Ambiguity is key here. Friends may go as far as to ask you what job you booked. It is encouraged to completely ignore them. Let those people assume you're taking time off to see the world (i.e. Dayton, Des Moines, and Schenectady).

Attaining an ideal sublet can be problematic. You want them to be connected enough to you that you aren't freaked out if they're going to trash your place and be late with rent, but you don't want them to be too close to you personally, that you feel guilty charging them more than the actual rent notated on the lease. It's a delicate balance. Perusing Gypsy Housing on Facebook will put you in contact with a person who has at least three friends in common with you that can vouch for them.

Compose a list of requirements you desire in a sublet and check in throughout your contract to verify they haven't crossed the line. Keep in mind that some people might be able to afford shelter – but you can't afford their tackiness. If you acquire a sublet that naively pays three hundred dollars over the rent, but when you visit on a layoff you open the door to a hallway lined with dorm room Christmas lights and pink Jesus candles, it might just be better to kick them out and cover the rent yourself.

Packing. Schmacking. A Regional Life.

Second order of business will be mastering the art of efficient packing. If you are working regionally, the company will be required to pay for (sometimes) up to one hundred pounds of shipped boxes *plus* two suitcases. That's two hundred pounds of fun and freedom for you to enjoy on your three-month getaway. Take advantage of it! You can start pulling out crap you haven't seen in years to send to your destination – just because you can. I'm talking *everything*. Snorkel gear. Snowboarding equipment. You just never know if you'll need that shit. Grab the thirty-percent completed scrapbook from the vacation you went on three years ago, toss in the guitar you keep in storage that you've never played, and don't forget your vaporizer or your bike. If you don't have a bike, buy one and ship it. Another option is to not ship anything outbound on the off chance you go antiquing with the cast and find a sweet chiffonier you want shipped home.

Packing. Schmacking. On Tour.

If you're going on tour, chances are you will only be allowed two checked bags weighing no more than fifty pounds each. Considering you will be on the road and disconnected from life for a fleeting three hundred and sixty five days or so, it seems only natural that you should be allowed the same amount of luggage that would typically accompany you on a trip home for the holidays. I suggest devoting one checked bag to toiletries and shoes, and the other to clothing. Your carry-on will be filled with anything you couldn't fit in your suitcases because you over-packed. It's inevitable that you will over-pack. You'll over-pack so badly that you'll need to ship a box home, because you'll simply have to buy that opening night outfit in your first city. By the fourth city, you'll be so sick of your clothes that a bi-monthly Forever 21 or H&M shopping binge will be essential to your sanity. It won't seem out of character, because those are the only two retail establishments economical enough for you to pretend you're getting an entirely new wardrobe – and not feel guilty when boredom sets in and you throw everything away five cities later.

You might also be provided with a trunk that the

company travels for you. In the olden days, a trunk really meant something. It was huge. It could carry a memory-foam mattress topper and a case of Trader Joe's Three-Buck Chuck. More importantly, it was delivered to your hotel room. Today, a trunk is actually referred to as a "footlocker" and it's roughly akin to the size of the cubby where you shoved Nintendo Valentines and Funyuns back in Kindergarten. The footlocker forever lives in the theatre and nobody is going to assist you in getting it to and from anywhere functional. If you put a lot of heavy crap in your footlocker, kindly ask someone to assist you in getting it down from wherever it lives. You don't want to tear your rotator cuff trying to locate a spare tub of protein powder. My theory is that the money saved transporting a smaller complementary luggage carrier is set aside for the workers' comp required to assist injuries resulting from the inability to retrieve said complementary luggage carrier.

Throwing Your Own Rager!

Your final and most important order of business before hitting the road will be to throw a balls-out-celebratory-going-away-bash. Don't look at this so much as a farewell party, but more like a formal announcement of your future employment. Make sure you invite everybody. Pack 'em in. It doesn't matter if you're leaving for three months or forever. You'd be surprised how many people that you haven't seen in years are willing to buy you celebratory drinks for getting a job, when they're unemployed. What can I say? People want to bask in your #blessedness!

When planning your party, make sure to take the Goldilocks approach with nearly every detail. For example, location is often a deal breaker for many people. You need to find a happy medium in an effort not to alienate anyone. The location can't be too obscure and inconvenient, but you don't want to be just another asshole that settles on Bourbon Street in Midtown. If someone gave me a dime for every time I've opened up a Facebook invite and grumbled, "Eww, Midtown," I'd have a lot of dimes. The venue has to be just right. Make it central enough so that nobody can complain about having to take a Brown Line train, but just far enough away from the Theatre District that you won't run into people you don't like, but also close enough to Broadway that the post-show crowd can't make excuses to douche out on you. Fuck it… You know you're just going to end up at Hourglass.

Time is of the essence. Schedule your party early enough so that the few weird people you know with day jobs and life goals don't decline, but late enough so you aren't obliterated by the time the second wave of partiers arrive. Nine p.m. is nice. Seven is for losers and eleven is for assholes. A middle ground is best, because it allows your party to flow through two to three waves of people. The early birds won't have much in common with the night owls. Luckily, one group will transform into another as the party goes on, leaving the people present surrounded by others whom they will find relatable. You, however, will be forced to endure the awkward turnover period of around twenty to thirty minutes when you're stuck with that one random person who sort of latched onto your group after an audition two years ago when they heard everyone was going out for drinks. They'll be there all night and will probably share your cab home.

The one detail of your farewell event that should not split middle ground is the quality. Make it a #rager they'll never forget. This is the last time you're going to see ninety percent of these people for a while. Enjoy this precious time with the friends who normally only exist to you through Candy Crush requests. Try not to be put off if someone close to you opts for the Irish Exit and forgets to say goodbye. You'll see them whenever you fly in for a quick twenty-four hour audition turnaround – just remember to only text your real friends on brief visits, and go radio silent on social media.

***

Now that you've tied up loose ends, it's time to kick up your heels, hurl two fifty-pound suitcases down the four flights of stairs in your walkup, and hail a reimbursable cab out to LaGuardia or JFK, and whatever adventure that economy priced ticket intends to take you.

DRUNK HISTORY: THE NATIONAL TOUR

In the Roman Catholic religion, there are artifacts known as "relics." Relics are items closely associated with saints. If you are lucky, one day you'll meet someone who toured the country on a Full Production Contract, and that person is known as a

First-National Relic. If you come in contact with this rare entity, I suggest you spend significant time in its presence. The First-National Relic is sacred. They are an ancient national treasure. They existed in a time when people actually went on the road to save money. They indulged in superfluous luxuries they didn't even need. The First-National Relic owns an apartment. They may even own a second property in a foreign location such as The Poconos. The only confirmed whereabouts you can witness this endangered species in action is in whatever city *Wicked, The Lion King, Jersey Boys,* or *The Book of Mormon* is playing – where they hide safely within their holy sanctuary.

What events transpired to bring along the extinction of the Full Production Contract tour? Take a trip back in time with me as I attempt to transcribe the somewhat booze-hazy yarn I learned at Chelsea Grill, from a First-National Relic (who I'll lovingly refer to as Old Annoying Actor Friend) that used to drink at a place called Marlowe – which is now the Brazilian BBQ joint next to Joe Allen's on 46th Street.

The Fall of the First National

A Drunk-matic Tale Told in the Words of Your Old Annoying Actor Friend

In the past, when you were no more than a babe, I earned an enviable living out on the open road. In those days, you didn't go on tour to pay bills. You went on tour to buy timeshares. Now, your weekly tour salary is like the $200 you get in Monopoly when you pass GO, before rounding a corner filled with hotels. It didn't always used to be like that...

A Long Time Ago, in a Broadway Season Far, Far Away...

There once was a revival of *The Music Man*, directed and choreographed by Susan Stroman. It was nominated for a lot of awards, but it didn't win any – except one. The 2001 First National Tour of *The Music Man* holds the esteemed acclaim of being "The First Time a First National Touring Company Launched Non-Union." I think the cast was making about 76-trom-BONES a week. This pissed off everyone. Equity actors were picketing cities all over the country. Newspaper articles ran in local papers. There was even general outrage among non-theatrical folk for the injustice of paying actors so little to perform while charging premium ticket prices to audience members. *The Music Man* required a gigantic cast, and the producers felt that the only way to tour the show at all was to send out a non-union company for (allegedly) salaries as low as $450 a week, plus housing and a $35 per diem. Actors' Equity was certainly not going to agree for any of their valued union members to work under such conditions. HELL NO. Steps needed to be taken to ensure this did not happen to a First National Tour ever again.

A New Kind of Tour

When Actors' Equity was given the chance to co-develop a cheaper way for producers to send actors out on the road, they freakin' jumped on that shit. AEA was like, "Please don't send the tour out non-equity! *The Music Man* was a mistake and we know that! We'll do anything!" And that is when the very first Multi-City Ass Rape Tour was born. For now, we'll just call it *42nd Street*. The First National Tour of *42nd Street* launched in August of 2002 under the newly conceived "Special Agreement Tour Contract" (a.k.a. Special Agreement to Be Paid Shit) with a minimum weekly salary of $575. That sounds like music to my ears. Come on along and listen to, the Lulla-bye-bye of Your Dignity. It might seem like a lot of money if you only make $30 at the dairy – but the *42nd Street* tour was playing first-rate cities, including a sit-down at the Ahmanson in Los Angeles, while the exact same production continued to run on Broadway, where the cast made over twice the amount. But – hey! At least the tour was union!

Things weren't looking that dark yet, though. Hits like *The Producers* and *Hairspray* were going out Full Production, so there were still opportunities and reasons to go on tour. Plus, the novelty of being plucked out of a touring company to replace someone on Broadway was still an alluring possibility. There was always a chance you'd get "bumped up" because the show was still running in New York. Now, tours rarely launch until well after their Broadway doppelgänger has posted a closing notice. Somewhere, a stigma was developed that booking a touring production is not as good as booking the Broadway production. Never mind that often the creative team goes back to the drawing board to improve the show for the road and future regional licensing.

You're not going to appreciate that, because you're still wondering why it took you six auditions for the Broadway company to book the tour.

Contract Experimentation

By 2004, Equity started dabbling in "experimental" touring programs designed to accommodate the diverse economic conditions of each show that went on the road by offering different tiers of salaries and other compensations. Like any good taboo experimentation, our union (with its members' best interest at heart) bent over and firmly grabbed its ankles to Bottom for the producers – and we all woke up with crabs in our eyes. Actors' Equity's experimental phase in touring gave birth to the bastard Tiered Production Contract – and we're not talking a cool bastard, like Jon Snow. The Tiered Production Contract is full on Special-Ed-King-Joffrey-Inbred.

The Tiered Production Contract was a sexy excuse to keep a show union while paying actors an amount based off how well the producers thought a tour would perform financially. The formula to decide our pay cut was based off words like "presenter, "guarantee," and "Net Adjusted Gross Box Office Receipts." Now – I'm too drunk to explain what any of that means, but it sounds pretty bad. Basically, the level of the tier is reflective of the cost of running the show vs. potential money earned. Productions that either cost too much to run or aren't projected to make a lot of money, are often placed on lower tiers. Can you imagine if this theory were applied to Broadway productions? I mean like –

wouldn't *Scandalous: the Life and Trials of a Kathie Gifford Vanity Piece* have been Tier C based off its box office advance? Wouldn't *Spider-Man: Turn Off the Crazy* be Tier D based off its running cost? Why is this behavior acceptable on the road? Is it only a matter of time before Actors' Equity agrees to a tiered Short Engagement Broadway Contract? Is anybody listening to me? #jazzhands.

Along Came SETA

There were originally six tiered categories ranging from B to G. In 2008, it was discovered that by the time a production qualified for the bottom three tiers, it was sold to a producer who would tour it non-equity. That is when tiers E, F, and G spun off and became the SETA contract – which has since grown to six categories itself. When I say "spun-off," I'm not so much talking a spin-off like *Frasier,* but more like the kind of spin-off when three of the Golden Girls moved to Miami to run a hotel. If you don't understand that reference, then I'll go back to the "bastard" one. Tiered Production Contract Tours is to Special-Ed-King-Joffrey-Inbred as SETA Tours is to people who think they're too cool to watch *Game of Thrones*… God, I suck at this – um … The SETA contract is so horrible it has two more categories than cancer.

The SETA contract stands for, "Take a-SEAT-a Before You Read That Paycheck." It also stands for Short Engagement Touring Agreement. The name suggests it was developed for small productions that tour for a short time. Wrong! It applies to any open-ended tour that doesn't play a given venue longer than four weeks. So... Like... That's *every tour*. SETA was originally created to protect the integrity of the Production Contract. Production Contracts are negotiated between the union and producers before SETA, to prevent concessions granted in the SETA contract from creeping into the Production Contract. At some point in the process, the SETA contract clawed its dirty ass out of the sewer where it had been biding time and building strength crudding up mucous and feeding off pond scum – and slashed the shit out of the Production Contract.

Fuck It, Cheers!

It was around this time in the national touring downward spiral that I gave up, married an IATSE member, and moved to Jersey to sell real estate. I was like, "EFF THIS. I'll let the stably employed spouse provide, while I wait for Broadway to call again." On another note, if you ever want to know what's happening with that workshop or out-of-town tryout you did, talk to the IATSE guys. They know what theatre a show is going into before the theatre owner.

After I quit touring, I got a bit disconnected from how things went down between 2008 and 2011. I've even logged onto Google to fill in the holes and complete the code, but it's unclear exactly when the top three tiers in the Tiered Production Contract got the "Red Wedding" treatment. It's like – one day I woke up and the first national tour of *Memphis*, the Tony Award winner for Best Musical, was on a SETA contract, and I was like – WTF? SETA all of a sudden had a first, second, and third category. Pretty soon every tour was SETA. You know that when the *Les Miserables* tour goes out SETA, we're all screwed. Luckily, the "integrity of the Production Contract" is safe because IT DOESN'T EXIST ANYMORE. The only producers who send out Full Production Contract tours these days are just trying to share the size of their man parts.

Don't get me wrong; the SETA tour isn't all that bad. The top category's weekly salary is $917 less than Production Contract, but you get free housing! You don't get free housing in New York! You also get $48 a day to pay for food! I mean, you can buy groceries for one week from a single day of per diem – unless you get stuck in a hotel with only a refrigerator and a microwave, which is often. It's amazing how fast you can burn through $48 before dinner because you don't have a kitchen, and the thought of microwaving egg whites one more time is disheartening.

Actors on tour used to live off their per diem and bank their salary. I'm dating myself, right? In any given city, a healthy omelet, green juice, Panera lunch, and sensible dinner will put you well over your per diem – and god forbid you want a glass of wine or toke of reefer after the show. If you're without a kitchen on tour and want to save money, you're going to have to choose between your bank account and your body. Should you choose the former, then kiss your waist goodbye, because it's damn near impossible to maintain your physique and fit into your costumes when the only way to bank your salary is via Clif Bars and McDonald's. #whatididforlove.

SETA also allows you to travel forty hours a week (and up to ten hours a day) in a bus if it's necessary. There's even a clause in the contract that allows for twelve-hour travel days for every thirteen weeks – but they can be executed all at once if the producer wishes. That means that for every fifty-two-week period, you might have to endure a twelve-hour travel day, *four times*. I wouldn't sweat the long travel days. I'm certainly too old to sit in hip-flexion for ten hours after a five show weekend, but you should be fine if you allot some of that per diem to Epsom salt and a foam roller.

The Light is Getting Dimmer

While I could continue discussing why the present touring life isn't quite what it was in the past, I think it's important we look toward the future. The national tour contract tumbled down the slippery slope of desperation out of fear. We, as a union, seem to be afraid that if we stand our ground and try to get things back to the way they were, everything will end up non-equity. If that's the concern, then let me present you with an example of how a recent Equity tour, that in an effort to stay union, is not a lot different from the non-union tour that started this mess in the first place. Second place? #yes. #how. #hmm. #ugh.

In the fall of 2013, a national tour launched starring a household name that many people know from a famous 1960's – 70's TV show, but you might recognize from a show that was on the WB before it became CW – and if you don't know what the WB is, you're dead to me. To protect the integrity of this production, I'm going to change the name to something completely random. Let's just call it, *Shmello, Shmolly!* When auditions for *Shmello, Shmolly!* were first published on actorsequity.org, I was like, "Did I accidentally log onto The Onion? Is this sarcasm?" The tour of *Shmello, Shmolly!* was slated to go out on a SETA Category Six contract for $548 a week, in which it was to play a scheduled seventy-three cities in six months. A 2011 – 2012 non-equity tour of a different musical (*Shmiddler on the Shmoof*) played over ten cities less, in seven months. Was this for real? Was there actually a universe where a non-equity tour had less one-nighters than an Equity approved tour?

At $548 a week, it would be criminal for your agent to take 10% from your paycheck. Under the assumption they take only 5%, and you loose an additional 15% to taxes and 2% to dues, you're looking at banking around $427 a week. I'm still trying to figure out how potentially forty hours of travel, plus twenty-four hours of performances a week, is better than working two shifts at an average New York City bar for the same amount of money. All this talk about numbers is making me want to play a game of what the kids call #throwbackthursday, and compare the conditions of *Shmello, Shmolly!* with the 2002 non-equity tour of *The Music Man.*

2002 Production Contract Minimum
$1,250

Alleged Non-Equity Salary
$450 + Housing + $35 per diem

Percentage of Production Contract Earned
55.6%

2013 Production Contract Minimum
$1,807

2013 SETA Category Six Salary
$548 + Housing + $48 per diem

Percentage of Production Contract Earned
48.9%

Getting the Chance to Perform and Share Your Gift
Priceless.

Based off those calculations, the cast of the non-equity tour was closer to Production Contract than the Equity tour by 6.7%. If *The Music Man* took place today, under the same conditions, it would be making $121 more a week than *Shmello, Shmolly!* – if you adjust for inflation.

Obviously there are exceptions to consider; mainly that *The Music Man* was a big First National and *Shmello, Shmolly!* was never intended to be anything more than a small bus and truck. However, *The Music Man* caused so much of a stink in each city it visited *because* of the limited salary the actors were being paid. Union members picketed because it was non-equity, but the media made a bigger deal out of how little the actors were being compensated when the audiences were still paying premium prices. To add to the oddity of this entire situation, tickets for *Shmello, Shmolly!* are (in some cities) only ten dollars cheaper than the average ticket price of the next Production Contract tour that follows it. I think it's a little bit dated to keep blaming the economy, when the average ticket prices on the road are often more expensive than on Broadway – regardless of how high or low the tier of the contract. Audiences aren't being given a cut. Why should we have to take one?

If we keep allowing concessions just for job opportunities, it's only a matter of time before the SETA Category Six goes from being the exception, to the rule. We need to do something about it. And like any good member of AEA, I'm going to fight the only way I know how – by venting to you over cocktails and then never attending a meeting or voting in any union elections.

I'll drink to that… I could use another drink… Does anyone still wear a show jacket?

***

OLD TIMES IS HARD

It was at that moment when my First-National Relic completely blacked-out on the bar at Chelsea Grill. I appreciated their story, but isn't it just like the Old Annoying Actor Friend to highlight how much better life was when they were in their prime? Things might not be as good – but who are they to discourage us from following our dream of touring the country doing what we love?

If the SETA contract was only created to make jobs available for union members, then we should jump on those opportunities because it's a chance to perform! We should be #grateful. Performing gives our position within this business some credibility and validates our life choice. Even if the SETA contract is just a Sad Excuse To Act, you can still have a lot of fun – even if you can't afford to buy fruit when you're hungry in between shows. #workiswerk.

However, there were some valuable life-lessons about touring that I was able to deduce from what my Old Annoying Actor Friend mumbled through their boozy-delusional-fog. This business is a job. You go to a job to make money to support your life. When you go out of town, you forfeit your life, in an effort to have a better life when you get home. You don't go on tour because you want to see Scranton. If you have a valid reason to go on tour, then by all means, do it. If you're breaking out of the ensemble to play a role – go on tour. If you just got out of a relationship and need a distraction – go on tour. If you're a vagabond or right out of college, without an apartment, bills, or responsibilities – go on tour. Do not go on tour just to scrape by. If you go on tour, find the appropriate time to do so, know when to quit, and know when to make the decision never to do it again. Much like "swinging," touring credits on a résumé only take you so far before they risk becoming your identity within this industry.

5 BROADWAY: (DEBUT!)

Can't wait until Tangled and Glee comes to Broadway so I can make my broadway debut already

*

Congratulations! You booked your first Broadway show! You've worked and #werked, and you're finally #livingthedream. You're about to become a full-fledged proud member of the Broadway Community. That means multiple morning TV show press tours, BC/EFA events, Tonys, free cookies from Schmackary's, and only six months before you're completely over all of it. I can't tell you how personally proud I am of you, and I would be so #grateful if you devoted a few words in your Playbill bio to thanking me. You get like fifty now. You're in the big time!

You've dreamt of it all your life, but you never truly know what your Broadway debut will be like until you're face to face with it. Many different variables will affect the overall quality of your debut. The Cast. The Creatives. The Content. The Critics. These are all determining factors in whether or not you will enjoy going to work every day. This is the first time you'll be performing in an open-ended show in the city where you live. You're not living in a bubble this time. You get to do-kick, get-check, and then go home to real life. This is the closest you'll ever get to a normal 9-to-5 job, so your quest to stay #blessed is all the more important now. After all that hard work, it would suck if you ended up in a "what now?" situation. You want to love your job – and to love your job, you need to love the people you work with.

COMPANY DYNAMICS

The dynamics within your cast were set in motion before you even auditioned. It began with the contract, content, and creative team. The contract sets the stakes before the first Equity Meeting. A touring contract, for example, dictates that the company will be living in a bubble for the duration of the job. The bubble-effect places a subconscious objective within each company member's mind before the first rehearsal. There is a need to connect to each other quickly and positively, because the next several months will be spent in close quarters together, where they will be living, eating, shitting, and sometimes shitting where they're eating. This means a touring cast will immediately strive to be the poster children for best-friends-forever-and-ever-until-life-ends-and-we-die-so-let's-go-to-a-strip-club-after-the-show-in-this-strange-town-because-I'm-totally-

OK-with-that. This behavior is indicative of a long run on the road, which we've already covered. A long run on Broadway is somewhat different.

The long run on Broadway is not guaranteed, but is always the goal. A lot of really exciting things come with your debut, but some of those experiences can be watered down if the majority of your cast is just too cool for school. Like, if your cast is generally annoyed by having to perform on the Macy's Thanksgiving Day Parade, then I'm really sorry because your cast blows. The *negatives* cannot offset the *positives*. If the *positives* balance out the *negatives*, you'll be fine. But if your *positives* outweigh the *negatives* too much, you could end up being led blindly into a "drinking the kool-aid" situation – which will be covered later.

Are You a Good Debut, or a Bad Debut?

Let's consider that you're making your Broadway debut in a new show. The Production Contract is a *positive*, so your cast should already be in a good emotional place walking in the door. However, this job is in town, so there might not be an immediate necessity to connect with each other. In theory, you could all hate one another, and it wouldn't be a huge loss because you already have friends. The social success of your debut will hinge on the ratio of debuts within your cast balanced with the circumstances in which the rest of your cast made their debut. The cast member who made their debut in a show that flopped is probably going to be slightly more grounded than the cast member who debuted in a hit. The flop leaves scars that encourage idealistic behavior. The hit sets a high benchmark that breeds jadedness. The most eager veteran in your cast is going the one who made their debut as a replacement in a long running show where nobody could give two fucks – so they're super excited to be doing something fresh. Unless they debuted in *Wicked*. If that is the case, find out how long they were at the Gershwin Theatre, because I think the bitterness-by-association seeps in after three months. If they debuted in *Chicago*, and are under thirty, they'll probably approach your show with the giddiness of a teenager. If they debuted in *Chicago*, and are over thirty, forget it.

Broadway Bonding

One of Stephen Sondheim's ground rules of songwriting is, "Content dictates form." This principle can also be applied to cast morale. If the content being developed does not initially bond a company, the connection between cast members will suffer, or at least take longer to mature. We're living in an era when it's easier to spend a five-minute break on our phones than by actually talking to someone. I'll bet you're reading this on your phone right now. #thankyoufive. Cast members bond when they are thrust into situations where they are forced to connect. If you're in a production where your job is to get thrown through the air and caught by a guy you met three hours ago, you can bet you're going to learn a lot more about that person in a shorter amount of time, than if you only share a few tricky traffic patterns together. If the content does not dictate situations where the cast needs to form bonds in order for survival, then you're going to end up with a lot of phone chargers around the rehearsal studio.

If content is not bonding your cast, it is up to a common enemy to bring everyone together. If your director is a douche, then eventually your entire company will come together over that common enemy. The same goes for content. If the production sucks, and everybody knows it, chances are good that everyone will relate to each other over their mutual frustrations. It's perhaps the only positive thing that can come from a shitty situation such as your show sucking. Now, what do you do if your show is terrible and you're the only one who knows it?

Drinking the Kool-Aid

The phrase "drinking the kool-aid" found its way into pop-culture after the horrible massacre in Jonestown. It's now used within the acting community when a company is performing in a theatrical massacre that they are convinced is good. Drinking the kool-aid is dangerous and easy to get peer pressured into indulging in. I get it. You want to fit in with your cast, and sometimes that means siding with their enthusiasm, even if it conflicts with your own opinions. It will happen. You will one day be involved in a project that seduces you with its clunky book, plodding direction, remedial lyrics, and Dolly Dinkle choreography. You'll succumb to drinking the kool-aid because it's a long run and the only way to save your sanity while the monkeys running the show rearrange deckchairs on the Titanic. Drink up. Better to be positive for the inevitable short run, than to drown in negativity. Just make sure that under the façade, you know your show is a stinker. Pride yourself in your awareness, but suppress that shit around your cast – like a gay Mormon kid does *before* he moves to New York.

When it comes to outside the job, one must never admit to having drunk the kool-aid. Drinking the kool-aid may not be literal suicide, but it sure as hell is social suicide. That's why when discussing your show with friends, it's perfectly natural and recommended to let your true self come flaming out – like a gay Mormon kid does *after* he moves to New York. If you're in mixed company, and you don't want to offend your cast-mates, or be perceived as foolish to your friends, I suggest using the following key phrase when discussing your show, "Oh, you know… It's cute. It's not going to change the world. But it's fun!" That's the best way to box-step right out of an awkward situation. Remember: Never stressed. Always blessed. #lietoyourself.

If it's your Broadway debut, you are contractually obligated to drink the kool-aid. It doesn't matter how good or how bad your show actually is. Nobody in your company is going to judge you for being excited in your Broadway debut. What people *do* care about is the rookie who does *not* drink the kool-aid because he or she is too busy partaking in trendy cynicism. No matter what the cool kids are doing, it's never cool to be jaded your first time out the gate. Save that for your next rodeo! Your career is a marathon not a sprint. If it's not your debut, feel free to enjoy putting down your show in equal company – but never complain about your job to your unemployed friends. Bottom line – know your audience.

I DON'T READ REVIEWS

The subject of whether or not an actor should read reviews has been debated since Shakespearean times. I have no hard facts to back that up, but considering *The Merry Wives of Windsor* was like the first spin-off ever, I doubt the Bard picked up any reviews that may have come hot off the printing press, as his play could have been received like the *Joey* to *Henry IV*'s *Friends* (again, no facts to back this up). It wouldn't have mattered anyway. If post-show critical pans even existed, they would have been redundant. When Shakespeare's audience thought your show sucked, they fucking let you KNOW IT. The groundlings paid a penny for admission and if you didn't deliver, you got a mutton chop in the face. Today, audiences are civilized to at least wait until intermission to throw the proverbial mutton chop at your cyber-face in 140 characters or less.

There are a lot of well-adjusted actors out there who genuinely avoid as much as they can about what is written about them online. However, if that well-adjusted actor is an understudy who gets to go on, you can throw all that shit out the window because you know they're searching their name on Twitter during curtain call. There is a difference between "reviews" and "crap online." People who are paid to critique your show write reviews. They are professionals, and whether you agree with them or not, they're performing a paid job. People who really hate you write crap online. They hide behind their computer, and sanctimoniously sound off angry opinions in a pathetic quest to garner attention. I mean, who does that? LOL. Only losers! [Visit annoyingactorfriend.com for an archive of over twenty critical blogs about season two of *Smash*.]

There are also people out there who will write great things about you online. There are many smart theatre lovers who simply enjoy sharing their love of the art with people like them. There can be value in that. However, if I show you thirteen educated tweets and message board posts about how you #nailedit in a performance, and one tweet calling you #fattypantssingsflat – who wins? #fattypantssingsflat wins. Every single time. Avoid the troll altogether and fill your voyeuristic needs by reading shit people say about your friends' shows.

The Other Boards

If you do find yourself lost in the wilderness of online discussion, you'll need some advice to take with you along your journey into the woods – of crazy. There are three major outlets to peruse the plethora of show business bitching, moaning, and occasional complementing: All That Chat, BroadwayWorld, and Twitter.

I consider All That Chat to be the oldest theatre related message board because it mainly consists of people who were around before theatre even began. Located at www.talkinbroadway.com, All That Chat boasts a bevy of personalities that have seen every production, of every play or musical – EVER. And they saw it when it was done better. All That Chat is what happens when you give a time capsule access to the Internet. I'm sure there are frequent posters of all ages and genders, but I like to read every single comment written on All That Chat in the voice of a sixty-three year-old gay man sitting alone in his apartment surrounded by an uncomfortable amount of plants and a wall of cast albums – on vinyl.

All That Chat is ultra conservative about what is posted on their board. They moderate that shit like the government. Being a member of All That Chat is a privilege, not a right. One time, I actively tried to make a profile so I could rave about my remarkable understudying capabilities, but the process to sign up was more cutthroat than anything I'd ever experienced as an actor. Once you sign up, you have to go through a waiting period where they decide if they will approve you. I'm not kidding. There is actually a callback process. It's essentially a background check, and I think after that there's a blood test. Worst of all, access to All That Chat is not immediate. You have to wait like a day, *or more*. You can literally "catfish" an unsuspecting Florida chick on Facebook faster than you can get approved to discuss Broadway on All That Chat. That's right, folks. It's easier to anonymously ruin a human being's life than it is to talk about Carol Channing.

If All That Chat is the elderly, ultra-conservative audience member sipping cognac out of a snifter and complaining about how much better things used to be, then BroadwayWorld is the teenage, uber-liberal audience member hopped up on molly and gummy bears, complaining about how much better things used to be. Again, I'm sure BroadwayWorld members come in all shapes and sizes, but whenever I read a post on that website, it's in the voice of a thirteen-year old fanboy wearing an *American Idiot* t-shirt, who is dead-set on his convictions because he's friends with someone in the show, and by "friends with someone in the show," I mean, he saw the show forty-seven times.

BroadwayWorld don't give a shit. Type whatever you want. It won't get deleted. It's a fuckin' free for all over there. It's the most bizarre community of pre-teens proudly dictating opinions they so strongly believe to be fact, that as a reader you might actually start to believe them, until they devolve into communicating with only GIFs from *RuPaul's Drag Race*. It would be easy to blame youth for their behavior, but then you discover that some of the profiles have been around for ten years, and it's basically the same people from when you trolled in junior high school. There also seems to be an adolescent turf-war between BroadwayWorld and All That Chat. They refuse to refer to each other by name and instead prefer the He-Who-Must-Not-Be-Named approach by dubbing their enemy, "The Other Board." Broadway is serious, y'all. I haven't seen a rivalry that gay since Riff pas de bourrée-d onto Bernardo's knife. #BlessedSideStory.

There may come a time when you feel

compelled to create a user name and start posting raves about the project you're working on. WARNING: *They will destroy you.* All That Chat and BroadwayWorld bond over one common enemy: The Shill (and Lea Michele, they hate Lea Michele). Praising one's own work under an online pseudonym is known as "shilling," and a surefire way to end up picking a wedgie like you're a kid in a John Hughes film. The only way to shill without raising eyebrows is to have a username older than five minutes. They won't suspect you as much if it doesn't look like you registered yesterday. Just create one now, in case you have something to say in five years.

They Will Find You

As a performer, Annoying Actor Internet Law requires you to read anonymous online opinions about you, take them personally, and then complain about how all those people on the theatre message boards are stupid, even though their comments are secretly murdering you from the inside out. Even when you make a point to block yourself from the boards, you can't block yourself from the mentions on Twitter. Fans are great about tagging you in nice posts. You know who else is great at tagging you? People who hate your show. Refreshing the mentions on your Twitter page is like flirting with someone you know is great in bed but occasionally likes to take a dump on your kitchen floor.

In conclusion, you can avoid reviews, but they won't avoid you. You can even delete your Twitter account and donate all of your modern technology to non-equity kids, but you'll still find a way to attract negativity from the awkward stage door audience members. I'm talking about the fans that say shit like, "You look so much smaller on stage!" "You look so young! I had no idea how old you were." "I even loved you in that other show you did." And my favorite, "Screw The Times. Your show is good!"

There are two kinds of actors in this business, those who do not read reviews and liars.

GEORGE M. COHAN MEMORIAL HIGH SCHOOL

Once your show is up and running, you get to truly step back and take a look at how the area from 40th Street to 54th Street, between 6th and 9th Avenues, so closely resembles your high school campus. I would venture to say it's like a college campus, but that would suggest a more established maturity level spread out amongst a larger region, surrounded by a denser variety of people. Nope. The Broadway Theatre District is full blown high school all over again. There's even a freakin' #BroadwayProm. How's that for irony? You move to the big city in an attempt to break free of your adolescent past, and wind up right back where you started – except this time the gangs are dressed in imposter Elmo costumes, and at least at your high school the prom wasn't rigged.

I like to refer to the Broadway campus as George M. Cohan Memorial High School. George M. Cohan's statue stands proudly in the center of Times Square, where he judgingly scrutinizes tourists' decisions at the TKTS booth. George M. Cohan Memorial High School's alma mater is not sung as often as it should be, but I think you should learn it. I'm not going to say it's *not* set to the melody of the one from *Grease*, but you'll particularly enjoy the incredible crassness of the moment when I try to squeeze an extra syllable into the ninth line.

George M. Cohan Memorial High School Alma Mater

As I go travelling down to Broadway,
The MTA will aid me on my quest.
I shall not ever be un #grateful,
For thou shalt always be etern'lly #blessed.

When I seek rest from being jaded,
I will call out - And lose one eighth of pay.
I'll follow what Equity's stated.
For I am #SOBLESSED to be on Broadway.

Gypsy of the Years, Broadway.
Bares of Broadway.
We give 2% to Equity.

Through openings, Broadway.
Closings, Broadway.
We screlt, Broadway to thee!

Upper Classmen and Lower Classmen

Like any normal high school, the classes at GMC High are broken down into freshmen, sophomores, juniors, and seniors. It can be difficult to decipher which class you and your friends sort into. If you still live for your job, you're definitely a freshman. If you typically bring non-theatrical-folk friends into Yum Yum Bangkok VII around six o'clock on a Saturday and pretend you're shocked to see people you know, when you really just brought your friend there to show how popular you are, you fall between a sophomore and a junior. Allow me to elaborate…

Broadway Freshmen

These are all the Broadway performers who are super-duper excited about their job and irritatingly wide-eyed about everything that comes with it. They're big on social media. They converse with their fans. They volunteer for every event. They love Broadway no matter how long they've been working there.

Broadway Sophomores

They still love it, but kind of want you to believe they're a bit too cool for it – even though everything still thrills them. Remember sophomore year of real high school when you were so happy to not be a freshman anymore that you pretended to be more of a cool veteran than you were? That's the same here. The Broadway Sophomore is the actor who sees you across 8th Avenue and screams, "Hey, girl! You going to your stage door? I'm going to my stage door, too." They're nonchalant, but still want everyone on the street to know what they do for a living.

Broadway Juniors

They're kind of over it. They don't go out as much after the show. They don't play in the Broadway Softball League. They don't do much of anything except pretend they're freshmen. They put up the front that they still love performing on Broadway, but secretly they hate it. Perhaps they've been playing the game a bit too long, but haven't figured out what to do with their lives next – because college doesn't teach you what the hell to do once you make it to Broadway and then stop caring. The Broadway Junior is the actor you see bitching about you (or something else), as they're walking down the street and when they see you they're like, "Oh, hey girl! Whatsup?"

Broadway Seniors

They hate it. They don't care anymore. They're bitter. They're jaded. They complain about their job in front of friends who have trouble just getting callbacks. They need to do what every senior eventually does… Graduate.

***

Let the following campus map of the 2013 – 2014 Broadway school year be your guide. Where you sit on campus is crucial…

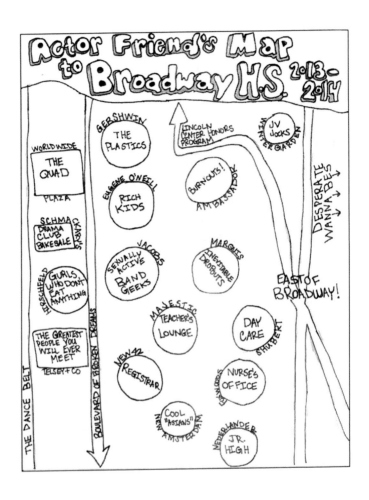

There is no age limit for each grade, or qualifications that need be fulfilled to move up or down within Broadway High School. You can be a freshman for your entire career. I doubt Elaine Stritch ever made it past sophomore year. On the flip side, I know a few people who've made their debuts as seniors. Once you've been admitted to this prestigious school, you never really leave. Even if you quit the business, you'll always be an alumnus whenever you go below 54th Street.

If your show closes, you're just being suspended, not expelled. Think of your unemployment period as a summer vacation while you anxiously wait for the next workshop or out-of-town tryout to bring forth a new #firstdayofschool. It's a cycle. Deep down, we're all just part of an incredibly supportive community that publicly roots for each other's success while secretly willing shows to close so we can take over their theatre. #LOvE.

6 FUNEMPLOYMENT!

dislike: waking up to texts from the well-meaning: "what show are you in next?" #funemployment #thanksforrubbingitin

*

It's time to experience life on the other side of the curtain. Believe it or not, there will come a time in your career when you are not exactly gainfully employed. Unless you are a government employee working at *The Phantom of the Opera*, *Wicked*, *Jersey Boys*, *Mamma Mia*, *Chicago*, or *The Lion King*, you should come to terms with the fact that all good jobs come to an end. This is not a cause for panic! This is a cause for celebration, because the great state of New York (or whichever state you worked in that has the highest maximum Unemployment insurance rate) is eager to pay you a weekly salary to audition – and by "audition," I mean, *day drinking!* And going to the gym at weird hours! Or watching your favorite TV shows before someone else spoils them! These are all magnificent reasons for your show to close. Sure, you'll miss the steady paychecks and Saturday Intermissions Pics – but wouldn't you rather have your #SIPs be of your feet, while lounging in Sheep Meadow? (NOTE: It's not *Sheep's* Meadow. The sheep never had possession of the meadow. They just used to hang out there before we took it over to #werk on our tans.)

There are times when Funemployment isn't always fun, but as long as you keep pretending you're on an extended vacation, you'll be less likely to judge yourself for lying on your couch in your pajamas at six o'clock in the evening. If you thought performing on Broadway was #livingthedream, then clearly your show has never closed, because the true dream doesn't even begin until after the final curtain. Before I dive further into how awesome Funemployment is, we should discuss how truly sick and twisted filing for Unemployment is…

FILING FOR UNUMPLOYMENT

Unemployment Insurance is temporary income for eligible workers who lose their jobs through no fault of their own. The money provided to you comes from taxes paid by your employer (IT'S FREE!). Figuring out if one qualifies for Unemployment can be tricky for actors because of the various jobs one might hold within a single calendar year. Deciphering the labor.ny.org website is easy enough if you have a college degree, unless it's a BFA (Bachelor of False Astuteness). Considering that I lovingly embrace my time on Funemployment, I am all too qualified and eager to break it down for you…

Qualifying for Unemployment

The Job: First, you must have worked somewhere that required you to submit your Social Security Number. That means 1099s do not apply. All those survival jobs (that we'll discuss later) will doubtfully make you eligible for benefits. In fact, if you try to claim on the $100 you banked dancing as a bear at the Paramus Park Mall, you'll probably get the company that hired you shut down and ruin it for all of us who rely on those weekend gigs to feed our families. Don't be an asshole. Do your research beyond my carefully constructed word vomit, and make sure you don't land you or your employer in prison. Orange might be "the new black," but "red" is the color of your pooper after prison rape.

The Circumstances: You must have been employed in a job that came to an end through no fault of your own. If you worked regionally, on tour, or on Broadway, and that show closed, then you most definitely qualify for Unemployment. If you were fired due to stealing from the folks in your dressing room, putting sugar in a cast-mate's makeup foundation, or being possessed by a South African demon that required the producers to ship in a shaman to perform an exorcism, then probably not.

The Time: The year is broken down into quarters. January – March. April – June. July – September. October – December. There are Basic Base

Periods and Alternative Base Periods. Your Basic Base Period is the first four of the last five quarters. The most recent quarter is not in your Basic Base Period. If your show just closed and you want to use those earnings, you can request an Alternative Base Period that considers the four most recent quarters. A show that ended in August of 2013 would yield a Basic Base Period of April 2012 – March 2013, and an Alternative Base Period of July 2012 – June 2013. Have you started eating your hair yet? Because we're just getting started...

You must have been employed in two different calendar quarters to qualify, and Unemployment will use the earnings from your highest quarter to decide the amount of your weekly benefits. One job is all you need, as long as it happened in two *separate quarters*. A Broadway gig over three months will do the trick. Or, you can collect a couple throughout the year. If you did a guest spot on *Smash* in Quarter 1 (January – March) and then worked at North Shore Music Theatre in Quarter 3 (July – September), and your job ended in August, you can file an Unemployment claim – but you have to wait until the beginning of Quarter 4 (October 1st) #FML. And you thought *booking* the job was the hard part?

The Amount: As of the date of this book's publication, the maximum benefits you can earn from the state of New York are $405 a week, for twenty-six weeks. That amount of cash is reminiscent of when you worked in dinner theatre, but without the threat of an octogenarian literally loosing their shit after your eleven o'clock number. To qualify for the maximum, the wages from your highest quarters divided by twenty-six (the amount of weeks you can claim) must average out to $405 or above. For example, say you booked the fall production at Paper Mill Playhouse in New Jersey. Their COST (Council of Stock Theatres) contract pays a minimum of $800 a week. Rehearsals begin in October, and the show runs through the end of the year. The entire job consists of ten weeks of work, but they are all within Quarter 4. Uh-oh. That's only one quarter and you need *two*. Hopefully you worked in another quarter within your base period, because otherwise you're screwed. [SIDEBAR: In Paper Mill's defense, they also produce productions that overlap into two quarters – but in doing so, the overall income you earned on the job is split. This leaves you fairly destitute, with a weekly Unemployment insurance benefit of like $47. Is there some sort of conspiracy going on between Paper Mill Playhouse and the state of New Jersey, where Chris Christie is guaranteed unlimited Turkey Gobblers from the Millburn Delicatessen, in exchange for MAKING IT DAMN NEAR IMPOSSIBLE TO EARN THE NEW JERSEY MAXIMUM OF $600?! (SIDEBAR WITHIN SIDEBAR: This is typically the case with all regional gigs ten weeks or under. I don't know what Chris Christie and sandwiches could possible have to do with the scheduling of a regional theatre's season – I was just hungry.)]

I digress… Let's pretend you also did a workshop during the month of March for *The House Bunny: the musical* at $631 a week. Bravo. You worked in two quarters. Since the $8,000 from Paper Mill Playhouse is in the higher quarter, it will be divided by twenty-six weeks, equaling an average Unemployment benefit of exactly $307.69 a week. Balls. To qualify for the maximum, you need to have made at least $10,530. I suggest finding another job that works around show schedules (LOL!). Let's pretend you book something that pays $3,000 and shoots on your day off. Don't ask me what. Make it up. Commercial, print ad, soft-core porn – I don't give a shit. If you think nobody is ever lucky enough to book two lucrative jobs that magically find a method to work around each other, then you obviously haven't met some of my friends.

Now that you have earned $11,000 in a single quarter, you can take that number and divide it by twenty-six. #Boom: $423. You've officially qualified for the maximum benefits of $405 a week for twenty-six weeks, and it only took you a shit-ton of patience, the scientific calculator option on your smartphone, and a degree from MIT. If you thought that finding a job that paid enough to qualify for maximum benefits was hard enough, then just wait until you get to file your claim.

Opening Your Unemployment Claim

According to the New York State Department of Labor (NYSDOL) website, "it is against federal and state law to discriminate based on race, religion, gender, marital status, age, disability, or political affiliation," but apparently not against people capable of common sense. Even if you follow their directions on how to file a claim with painstaking accuracy, it will most likely be for naught. Once you accept this fact, and come to terms with the reality that filing your claim could take anywhere from a few simple hours (if you're lucky), to weeks of soul-sucking frustration (if you're me), you'll be a much happier person. Moving forward, I want you to expect the worst, but allow yourself to be pleasantly surprised. That's kind of my thought process whenever I attend a Broadway show.

Near the end of your production's run, someone (usually from company management) will provide you with the company's EIN (Employer I.D. Number), which is also known as a Federal Tax Identification Number. You are now ready to open your claim on the NYSDOL website! It's so easy! All you have to do is log in, create your Government I.D., follow all the instructions, and you'll be rolling in four hundred and five George Washingtons faster than a Michigan alum can get everything they've ever wanted, right? WRONG. Just when you think your claim has successfully been filed online, you read the dreaded words, "Please call us to complete your claim." That's when a process worse than burning in the fiery pits of hell, or waiting in a student rush line, begins.

Getting a hold of an actual person from Unemployment on the phone is sort of like playing a reverse game of Russian Roulette, where only one chamber is empty, and you're stuck spending an afternoon repetitively blowing your brains out. Allow me to explain in detail what an average telephone relationship with the New York State Department of

Labor is like...

The following dramatization is based on true events and could easily happen to you...

You awake one cheery morning, feeling erroneously optimistic about your career, and twenty-six beautiful weeks of Funemployment. You've already filled out the proper online application to open a claim, so you proceed to complete the process over the phone as instructed. After dialing the number, you listen to a thirty-second speech from an automated lady who explains that you first need to log online to open your claim and you're like, "Shut the fuck up you stupid bitch, I already did that and then you told me I needed to call to finish it." My, how quickly a mood can change when faced with conflict involving one's income.

You take a deep breath, and continue listening to a series of prompts asking various questions that require you to press numerous buttons for what seems like an eternity – but in actuality is probably only twelve minutes. (HINT: Write down all the numbers you just pressed in that exact order. In the future, it will cut down your time dealing with the prompts by about five minutes. You'll value that shortcut, because you're going to get disconnected. A lot.)

After a rather arduous listening process, you are told that to complete your claim you need to call back on a specific day of the week that coincides with the spelling of your last name. Last names beginning with an A – G on Monday, H – N on Tuesday, and O – Z on

Wednesday. Names beginning with a consonant, but only have one vowel, must call on Thursday between 10:00 a.m. and 12:42 p.m. People who have to use a middle initial in their Equity Name must complete their claim every other Friday. Etc. Etc. Etc. You look at a calendar, because you're on Funemployment – and when has anyone on Funemployment ever known what day it is? Your heart sinks. It's Tuesday, and your allotted day is Monday. You will now be forced to wait an extra week without money.

The long week ticks by, while you try to ignore the absence of a paycheck by binge watching the latest in-vogue Netflix series. Monday arrives. You open your claim, and you're so bloody excited that it seems like a big #blessed rainbow is about to come beaming out your butt – but not so fast, George Banks! You still have to sit through the mandatory "one week waiting period." Two weeks. No money.

When Sunday-NO-Funday (because now you're broke) finally rolls around again, you're ecstatic because you've made it through two weeks without money, whilst surviving on PB & J and the happy hour at McCormick & Schmick's. You go to file online, but (plot twist!) something is wrong with your claim, and you need to call Unemployment to sort it out. Aren't you glad you kept those automated prompt numbers written down? Time to put them to good use. Honestly, that little piece of paper has been more helpful in my career as an actor than the semester in college that I spent annotating *Coriolanus*.

Monday morning, armed with the prompt list you constructed last week, you take a deep breath, pick up your phone, and call Unemployment – whose contact information has been begrudgingly added to your "favorites" list without a drop of irony gone unnoticed. You swiftly dial your way through the switchboard catacombs to a level where you might be #blessed by the presence of an actual human being who can assist you with your claim. Now, all you need to do is correctly answer the three riddles given to you by the minotaur that guards the Narnia closet hidden within the Coca-Cola refrigerator at the Hot & Crusty in Penn Station, and you're well on your way.

Once you find an option to link you to a live representative, one of the following three possible incidents will occur:

POSSIBILITY #1: An automated voice will explain, "We are experiencing an abnormally high volume of calls. Please call back later. And also, go fuck yourself." CLICK. GAME OVER. RESET.

POSSIBILITY #2: An automated voice will explain, "We are experiencing an abnormally high volume of calls. All of our representatives are busy today. We can schedule you an appointment for a callback."

This option is hysterical, because it's at that moment when you realize you even need a "callback" for Unemployment. So, you select the "callback option" and they say, "The soonest we can schedule you an appointment is Thursday."

But you're like, "It's Monday. How can Unemployment be booked solid until Thursday? Is it 2008? Fine. I'll wait until Thursday."

Next, the computer asks you to select the time to call you back, and you say, "How about ten in the morning?"

"We're sorry. That timeslot is full."

"Eleven?"

"We're sorry. That timeslot is full."

"Noon?"

"You've exceeded your number of options today. Goodbye." CLICK.

After this happens, I suggest scheduling some extra time in your week to take your iPhone to the Apple Store, so they can fix the cracked screen caused from being Frisbee tossed across a studio apartment. Even when you finally do get to schedule a callback time for later in the week, take a long look at the alcoholic beverage you undoubtedly poured during this process, and accept the fact that the glass is half empty, because this is all in vain. What are the odds they're actually going to call you back on your scheduled day?

Still, when it comes to the measly weekly penance the government gives us to spend hours at Pearl Studios reassessing our life choices, we're all just Charity Hope Valentine, and the New York State Department of

Labor is some slob sweating gin and throwing dimes at us while we taxi dance, believing our phone call will actually come – because there's gotta be something better than this.

Thursday morning arrives. You wake up extra early (like before noon) and you wait by that phone. At this point you've gone three weeks without money and you're like, "I'm not gonna miss this shit!"

An hour passes. Two. Three. It's now six o'clock, they close at seven, and this call is eight hours late. So, you say #fuckit and call them back to start the entire grueling process all over again.

Listen. If Unemployment offers to call you back on a different day, you will never get your callback. Broadway will call. Your pilot will get picked up. Your ex-significant other will realize the error of their ways, and come crawling back to you. But Unemployment is *never going to call you back.*

POSSIBILITY #3: Winning the lottery! This is the option in the demented game of Unemployment Russian Roulette where you hear the click of an empty chamber, and not the click of the other line hanging up on you. You've won the Power Ball, folks. Savor it when you hear the words, "We are experiencing an abnormally high volume of calls. You can either *wait on the line for the next available representative, or we can call you back when it's your turn.*"

Now, you're probably thinking, "This can't

possibly be a good thing, right? I could be on hold for hours, or worse, relinquish my spot in line under the foolish hopes they might call me, thus placing me right back at the start!"

I promise, you will not lose that place in line. Your number will be taken down, and if they say they will call you in twenty-three minutes, they will indeed phone back in twenty-three minutes. It's amazing! They actually do that. Deciding who gets the Holy Grail of Unemployment Phone Options is some Illuminati bullshit I'll never quite understand – like the Twitter verification process.

***

Once you've finally made it through to a person who can help you with your claim, you can ask them what witchcraft is being done to your Unemployment benefits. They'll probably say something like, "That random state you worked in hasn't reported your wages yet."

And you'll naively ask, "Can I call them?"

"No," responds NYSDOL Dip Shit #1.

"Can *you* call them?"

"No."

"Then what can *I* do?"

"Wait until they report it."

Since it's been three-plus weeks of waiting, this little hiccup is pretty much just a blade of grass in the football field of worst-case scenarios. You decide that a few extra weeks (and a couple thousand more phone calls) aren't going to do much harm before that rogue state finally reports your wages, and you're presented with a retroactively paid dinosaur-dump-sized-lump-sum, that I strongly suggest you get the taxes taken out of – unless you have some sadomasochistic attraction to the words, "you owe state and federal."

You can take a deep breath now. The hard part is over. It's time to sit back, relax, and enjoy twenty-six weeks of...

LIVING A LIFE OF LEISURE

The quality of your Funemployment is not only going to be measured by what kind of jobless lifestyle you like to live, but by what season you're stuck living it in. If you're unemployed between the months of May and September, then not only have you found a way to dodge summer stock, you're going to be a touch more mentally stable than if you find yourself with nothing to do during the winter – which usually takes place in New York between Labor Day and Memorial Day.

Summer in New York is glorious. It doesn't even matter that for three weeks, the entire city morphs into a nine-mile inferno that generates a smell not unlike what would happen if you entrapped a touring bus full of fart enthusiasts inside a Las Vegas food court. Who gives a shit? It's summer! The days are long and – TANK

TOPS! Your friends may have money to go on vacation, but it won't matter because you'll *look* like you just spent a week in Aruba. Plus, there are hardly any auditions, so you don't have to feel guilty about being a complete loser for spending most of the week in Sheep Meadow doing a handstand – or discovering yet another bottomless brunch establishment, where you can drown your jobless sorrows in Bloody Marias with the only three friends you know who aren't at Sacramento Music Circus, the MUNY, or an undisclosed theatre in New England where their weekly paycheck after taxes and agent fees is equal to your Unemployment benefits. Meanwhile, your locally employed friends will be burdened with crap like Tonys rehearsals, Broadway in Bryant Park, and paying for drinks at bars after the happy hour ends. Besides, they won't be spending much time with you anyway, because they'll be too envious of the exclusive relationship you're having with your DVR – as well as your perpetual, stomach-turning fear of the future!

Winter in New York City is the antithesis of anything in your life that has ever made you happy. Don't be fooled by the joy surrounding the Macy's Thanksgiving Day Parade, the lighting of the Rockefeller Christmas Tree, or the hopeful thoughts that naturally develop within your heart when the ball drops in Times Square. Those are fleeting seasonal distractions that only mask the inevitable ice-hell you're about to plummet into and be held prisoner within for the next four months. You're going to be cold. You're going to be broke. You're going to attend ECCs. You're going to get face-raped by your friends who went out west for pilot season and enjoy repetitively reminding you that there aren't seasons in California. You'll find yourself drinking at four o'clock in the afternoon because it's dark out and just seems natural. You'll eventually start looking for excuses to justify why you don't have to go to an audition, because just the thought of venturing outside into the frozen tundra with a dance bag, to risk slipping on subway steps laden with two-day old snow sludge that vaguely resemble piles of Dairy Queen's Oreo Blizzard, isn't nearly as unpleasant as encountering a working friend in Hell's Kitchen. You'll discover that there are only so many times you can watch *Home Alone* before you realize that if you were to die right in the middle of the film, it would not go unnoticed because your Facebook friends would detect an absence in your incessant social media activity well before, "Kevin! What did you do to my room?!"

If it all possible, try not to find yourself on Funemployment in the dead of winter – unless you know how to combat seasonal affective disorder, or if you're cool with your liver eventually resembling the pelt of a snow leopard.

After all is said and done, do not let the time frame of when your Funemployment occurs derail you from maximizing your life of leisure. If things go horribly wrong, and you don't book a job immediately, you're looking at over six months of sort-of paid vacation. When people ask what you're up to, tell them, "Taking some much needed time off! Things were just so crazy for a while!" Don't let on that you're secretly dying inside. Anxiety is so dated! If you approach living a life of leisure on Funemployment as if the circumstances are something you actively sought out, you'll be one step closer in mastering how to use self-deception as a method to success.

SURVIVAL JOBS

This may come as a complete shock, but I have on an occasion found myself without Unemployment insurance, and thus had to perform various odd jobs around The City and Tri-state area to pay my rent, feed myself, and find an acting job that I'm proud to discuss publicly. I've heard rumors that some actors actually collect Unemployment while working "under the table" jobs – BUT I DON'T KNOW WHAT YOU'RE TALKING ABOUT I'VE NEVER DONE THAT.

When you #werk as hard as I do, you tend to play a little harder, and that requires you to WORK even harderer. Here's a list of just a few of the employment opportunities that I've been #grateful to perform while #livingthedream:

Professional Retail Sales Associate

I unpacked, stocked, and sold clothes and other accoutrements for a sample sales company. One time I folded sweaters next to a future Tony nominee who was standing next to a former Tony nominee that was selling a scarf to a Tony winner. Strap on a bib, kids, because The Universe can serve up a mean shit-sandwich, and it's only a matter of time before we all get to take a bite.

Private Event Entertainer

Mikhail Baryshnikov takes dance class whenever he can. If you are not being paid to dance eight times a week, I suggest you do the same. Not only must you be in prime condition when auditions pop up, you also want to make sure you're agile enough to #werk the dance floor at an occasional bar mitzvah or other multi-million dollar event. Do you like Gatsby themed parties? Well, you're in luck, because you just might be invited to one at the lavish Waldorf Astoria, where the guest of honor isn't Nick Carraway, it's a pre-pubescent Jewish boy who is celebrating the completion of his coming of age rituals while you do the Charleston on a temporary stage surrounded by six hundred thousand dollars worth of orchids and a group of teenage girls who won't stop making fun of your costume. Just when you begin to wish that someone would put you out of your misery (bringing the job to a self-referential end, befitting of the party's theme), you remember that the check will clear and you need never speak of it again.

You'd be surprised how much money people have to burn on live, human decorations, in an effort to create a desired party atmosphere. I've seen them all. I've done them all. No matter how different each event might be, the common staple is always the drunken middle-aged rich lady who wants to dance with you whether you're gay, straight, male, or female. Pretty much all of the women at these parties are Kathie Lee Gifford at different stages in her life.

Some of my more memorable jobs include the

time I sock-hopped for a 1950's themed charity auction at some single millionaire's mansion in Long Island where the house was so big he didn't know what to do with half the rooms so he just kept them empty with the doors closed. I've greeted guests as they entered a party in New Jersey, and then posed for pictures with them wearing one of those out-of-a-plastic-bag disco Halloween costumes that you find at Ricky's. I could go on, but the rest of the list pretty much includes more events involving multicolored full body onesies than I care to admit. #fame. #broadway. #whatididforlove.

Alcohol Enthusiast

I worked as a bartender where my interest in alcohol was showcased nightly, and like any good stereotype, I also waited tables, where my enthusiasm toward alcohol was mainly observed by "spilling a guest's drink" on the way to their table – yet somehow finding a way for it to end up getting consumed in the stairwell after it was voided off the check.

The juxtaposition between waiter and bartender is not unlike that of an actor and a casting director. When you're behind the bar or the table, you have the power. Someone wants a drink. Someone wants a job. They have to go through you to get it, and that provides you with respect. When you're on the other side, taking a table's order or auditioning for a role, it's like the fucking trenches. If you can find a way to manipulate the power back to your side, then maybe you'll walk out with a callback – or survive the night with an 18% tip average (15% if you got hit with a lot of Europeans).

Online Personal Ad-venturer

When things are *really* slow, I've been known to peruse the Craigslist ads for odd jobs around town. If you reach this point in your life, I suggest reevaluating exactly where you've placed the bar for yourself. It'll be better for your mental health if you lower it just a bit. Who knows? What once seemed like rock bottom, might be a blessing in a severely perverted disguise. I'm not saying to do porn. But, like – there are people out there who will pay you to do shit like hide Easter eggs in their apartment. If that means free candy and the opportunity to be in The City for auditions, then why not? You just need to balance how you value your time and dignity. For example, would you rather spend forty-five minutes taking part in a fetish video dedicated to fully clothed girls being carried around, or make the same amount schlepping about the country doing one-nighters on a tier double DD touring contract? Which of those two career choices eats less away at your soul? Sometimes it's better to venture into Prospect Park on a Tuesday afternoon to participate in a sensible cradle lift for three hundred dollars cash, if it allows you to be in town the next time *Mamma Mia* holds replacements auditions.

Theatrical Advertising Agent

Yeah, I did it. I wore a sandwich board in Times Square. And you know what? Of all the jobs previously mentioned, this one provided me with health benefits – and they were easier to attain than through Actors' Equity. To be #blessed with Cigna (second only to SAG-AFTRA's health insurance as far as badass co-pays are concerned), one must work twelve weeks within twelve months under an Equity contract to acquire six months of coverage, and twenty weeks to earn a year. You are then evaluated quarterly, so if you work twelve weeks, but they are split between two quarters, you will have to wait until the end of the following quarter to begin your six months of coverage. That gives you ample time to experience a credit card and career crippling accident. If you must get hurt or sick, make sure it's on the stage, where workers' comp can cover it. At least when I was dodging cabs, Cookie Monsters, and Chicago Flyer Girls in Times Square, I knew that a violent altercation with any one of them wouldn't result in years of debilitating hospital bills.

Furthermore, this job actually required me to pull out crap I learned in my BFA program to sell tickets to the shows I represented. My vast knowledge about Sondheim, Rodgers, Hart, Kern, the Princess Musicals, and shit like *Your Arms Too Short to Box with God*, made it easy to explain to tourists from Ohio why the musical emblazoned on my constricting double-boarded prison was a good fit for them. It was instrumental to my success that I knew what I was doing. I'm not really certain the same applied to landing a job in the show I was advertising. Still, it was nice knowing that over one hundred thousand dollars was spent on my education, and none of it ever went to better use than right smack on Broadway – between a McDonald's and the guy who asks, "Do you like comedy?"

SIMPLY SURVIVING

In this business, surviving is just as important as thriving. "Success" is so often defined by how much money you make. I say, "fuck that," and find your own version of "success." Broadway might be your benchmark, but sometimes success is making it through the day without breaking down into the Oprah Ugly Cry to an Adele album. Success can simply be your personal contentment with where you are in life at that given moment. If you take pride in how you make it to the next day, then you are achieving success.

Funemployment is a balance between money, pleasure, inconvenience and happiness. If you weigh pleasure and happiness unevenly against money, you may end up an everlasting couch-hopper – and that could be pretty inconvenient. If you compromise happiness and pleasure in favor of money, you might spread yourself too thin, and end up burning out right before your next big break – and that would be pretty inconvenient, too. Consider your alternatives, and find out what work will make you #werk. If accepting a certain survival job is going to compromise your happiness, eat Top Ramen for a week and look for other options. Find what's best for you. Sometimes it's better to perform a twelve-minute make-out session with a statue in Central Park for an agalmatophilia fetish video, than to miss Thanksgiving with your family to work a catering job because it's socially acceptable.

Don't get discouraged if you wait longer than is desired before landing a "conventional" theatre job. All survival jobs draw from your acting background. It's just a matter of how you look at it. You might not be aptly qualified to sell designer wear, dinner specials, fine wine, baby clothes, etc., but if you use your natural born acting ability and *pretend* like you know what the hell you're doing, you'll get the job done. Even if things reach the point where you consider hopping on a stripper pole once or twice, at least you'll be #grateful for all those ballet classes! And sometimes working a job that your nine-year-old-self didn't necessarily dream about every night can find a way to surprise you. Honestly, I'd trade some of the mediocre productions I've done with casts that never clicked, for the gratification I've felt after expertly tour guiding a couple celebrating their anniversary through a three-course meal, backed by a wait staff that would gladly throw themselves in front of a bus to make sure my guest's cappuccino made it to the table before the foam fizzled. Some of the greatest people you'll ever meet are actors in between jobs.

7 SOCIAL NETWERKING ETIQUETTE

***All this hard work over the years is paying off!
B4 age 25, I have toured the world, won major
awards and on my way to Broadway!! #Blessed***

*

By now, you've been #blessed with a wonderful career in show business. However, you cannot be #SOBLESSED until you learn the art of Social Netwerking. *Netwerking* is the single most important element of #werking in this industry. Henceforth, I will refer to it as *netwerking*, because a sensitive subject such as this must be treated as preciously as a summer callback. Your ability to present the ultimate fabricated version of yourself will be key when it comes to mastering this subject.

Sometimes you can't make it to every single gypsy run, BC/EFA event, or concert with a cover charge and two-drink minimum. A lot of netwerking goes on at those events. If you can't be at one, find a way to include yourself via social media, while standing in the back of the event you're actually present at. It's important to over-saturate yourself. That is why I suggest you create profiles on the three most popular social media websites: Facebook, Twitter, and Instagram. This is known as the Trifecta of Social Media Excellence (not to be confused with the Trifecta of Broadway BFA Bountifulness, which means your current show hosts cast members from CCM, CMU and Michigan). For the Trifecta to be tri-ffective, you must make certain that every single thing you post online is funneled through all three social media sites. If not, then you're basically just wasting everybody's time. Your picture means shit to me unless I see it on Instagram via a tweet that I've clicked off your Facebook page.

Once you've created your new social media empire, you might be wondering, "How do I effectively showcase my #werk so I can book more work?" I'm glad you asked, because I have compiled hours of tiresome research and practical application to develop the Quintessential Annoying Actor Friend's Guide to Behaving on Social Media. Let's begin!

1.
<u>CHOOSE THE RIGHT WORDS</u>

bless·ed *adj.*
1. a. Worthy of worship; holy.
 b. Held in veneration; revered.

Constructing a proper tweet or status update is akin to crafting an intricate lyric. It's all about the words.

Stephen Sondheim once said, "I've always thought of lyric-writing as a craft rather than an art, largely a matter of sweat and time." I relate to this because when I tweet, "#blessed," it's not just an off-the-cuff hashtag, but rather the product of tedious rewrites meant to evoke empathy for my self-appointed holiness. Actors are like the Sondheims of social media!

When choosing a hashtag to properly articulate how #lucky one feels about their good #fortune, actors steer clear of options like #advantageous, #propitious, or #opportune. Instead, we lean in favor of the most revered adjective in the English language: #blessed. It's the only word to appropriately describe how I feel whenever something fantastic and worthy of envy happens to me. However, trends come and go so quickly around here. What was once "fierce" is now "everything," and while it's great to honor the classics, perhaps it's time to move on. Millennials are forward thinkers, right? The simple act of plugging #blessed into Thesaurus.com blew my mind with a plethora of synonyms that could really push the envelope in social media #gratefulness. Think of how of how groundbreaking it will be when we start trending hashtags like: #adored, #sanctified, #divine, or #amongtheangels.

The Future

I love my cast! I feel #consecrated.

Someone donated to my Kickstarter! I'm being held in such veneration!

What a great audition week! #SoySacrosanct

2.
<u>USE STOCK PHRASES</u>

Actors are very busy people. Sometimes we are not afforded the hours in the day that staff writers on television shows are given just to be creative. So, when you take to social media to share your awesomeness, you should rely on stock phrases to save time. Here are a few of my favorites:

Remember That Time?

This is a great one to use whenever you want to share some kickass news, but are trying to be coy about it. It sets the status up nicely, too! You don't want to be too abrasive by taking to Facebook with:

I just did a screen test for HBO!

Do you see how desperate that sounds? It's much classier to say:

Remember that time I did a screen test for HBO?

Isn't that a much better choice? Even though your friends will actually have no recollection of you doing a screen test for HBO because it *just happened*, they will, for reasons unbeknownst to anyone, click the LIKE button.

I'm a big fan of *Remember That Time?* because it's casual and shows people that whatever just happened to you is…

No Big Deal (NBD)

This phrase is key when you want to share some wonderful news, but are short on time and need to remain as blasé as possible. You don't even have to start out with a *Remember That Time?* (but you can). Simply toss in an "NBD" at the end of your tweet. It's even better if you hashtag it! For example, don't say –

THE Liza Minnelli said the show was terrific!

That sounds juvenile… like you still do lottery for *Wicked*. Try this instead –

Liza came backstage to tell me she enjoyed my performance. #NBD

That sounds more mature…. your friends will respect you for it!

NBD is a great standby, but I think it's best saved for personal encounters with celebrities. Using an #NBD after receiving a callback or booking a job doesn't #werk. That situation calls for a…

When it Rains, it Pours!

We all know that success finds safety in numbers. When you book a job, you're probably going to book four more, and they're all going to conflict with each other. Since you won't be privileged to place all these jobs on a future résumé, the only way to share the credits that will never be is to blast *When it Rains, it Pours!* on social media. If anything, you get the opportunity to let your unemployed friends know that booking jobs is just as frustrating as *not* booking jobs.

That Moment When ...

This actor-fave-phrase is similar to *Remember That Time?* but is just a bit more sentimental. You want to reserve a *That Moment When* for when something really special happens to you. Like dreams-come-true special. A *That Moment When* is incomplete without a #blessed, #grateful, or something involving #dreams. They go together like bacon and eggs, Bloody Marys and a Monday, or me and a final callback for the creative team. Here is how to use it in a sentence:

That moment when William Morris agrees to meet with you. #daretodream

That moment when you find out you're taking over as Elphaba standby. #thankyoutelsey

That moment when you remember you're on Broadway. #blessed

-- Said No One, Ever

The origins of this statement appear to date back to that one week in the beginning of 2012 when everyone put on their "I'm-Exceedingly-Funny" hats to lampoon their job, hometown, or favorite hobby, by posting a *Shit BLANK Says* video on YouTube. These videos consisted of a slew of inside jokes quoting what people within the given subject say on a daily basis. There was everything from *Shit Girls Say* to *Shit Theatre Girls Say* to *Shit Theatre Girls Who Are Singers Who Move Well Say*.

While the *Shit BLANK Says* videos eventually went the way of the Harlem Shake and flashmobs (I miss those! – Said No One, Ever), one of the more popular entries, *Shit Nobody Says*, has since evolved into a witty tag at the end of a statement that nobody believes to be true. And let me tell you, THAT SHIT KILLS!

If you're ever starved for a good social media gag, I suggest coming up with a ludicrous declaration and then attach, *Said No One, Ever* at the end. It will never fail to be the source of great hilarity! Example:

Eight shows a week is easy! – Said No One, Ever

Walking residual checks to the bank is annoying. – Said No One, Ever

I hate callbacks!!! – Said No One, Ever

This approach is failsafe because not only are you making a funny joke, you're also discussing relatable topics and keeping your friends informed about how you're doing – and they'll be #grateful to hear!

Sondheim Lyrics

Sometimes your own words aren't able to articulate what you want to say. If that is ever the case, just quote a Sondheim lyric at random. Preferably one from *Into the Woods* – in fact, you should probably only use lyrics from *Into the Woods*, because if you pull something out from *Pacific Overtures* your friends will find you pretentious.

My favorites include, "The slotted spoon can catch the potato," because it's a subtle and ambiguous way to tell everyone that you booked a job without having to actually say it. "Excited AND scared," is great for #firstdayofschool – but don't forget to caps lock the AND. It doesn't work if you don't. Finally, "Is it always OR? Is it never AND?" is an awesome alternative to *When it Rains, it Pours*

3.
<u>STRIVE FOR AMBIGUITY</u>

The only thing more effective than posting a casting announcement of the latest job you booked, is prematurely posting a status that evokes the age old question, "What the hell did they book?" One of the most annoying things about working a lot is that you have to wait a very long time until casting is official before you can share your good fortune with your friends. Often, you'll be like two weeks into rehearsal before they bother to announce the cast on Playbill.com. So, what happens when you get the call from your agent and you just can't wait? I certainly don't give a shit if I've signed a contract or if the theatre is even booked. I NEED TO SHARE! Luckily, there are ways around this tricky subject that can get your news out into the ether without sacrificing your reputation with the production.

Book a job? Try this!

Such good news! Wish I could share. #staytuned

Book two? Stay humble.

Wow. Speechless. Hard work really does pay off. #blessed

Important callback? Put it out in The Universe!

Positive vibes at 5:10p.m. please!!!

There are numerous other ways to remain ambiguous while still getting your point across. Be creative! Have fun! If your friends LIKE your status and respond with questions like, "WHAT HAPPENED?" or "Deetz, please!" then you've done exactly what you set out to do.

4.
<u>SHOW A LITTLE SKIN</u>

All actors realize that physical fitness is important to overall health, as well as overall employment. I should know, because I'm practically at the gym all day long! Being the best version of you is something I cannot stress enough. I once thought that showing gratuitous skin died in the great NYC Soap Opera Slaughter of 2009 – 2011, but it only got worse. There's still HBO, Showtime, AMC, FX, MTV, Nickelodeon, etc., and they want to see so, so much more. They want to see your ass, and they want to compare your ass with the asses out in Hollywood. That means you're essentially competing with PVC pipes for a partially nude under-five.

So, what do you do when your body is #nailingit but you don't necessarily nail your audition? Who is going to appreciate all your hard #werk? Did somebody say GYM SELFIE?! #bingo. It is absolutely appropriate to lift up your shirt in front of one of the mirrors at your gym and snap a pic of your stomach. Nobody within your chosen fitness facility will find that weird at all. Next, upload it to Instagram and pick a filter. I recommend Brannan or Lo-Fi for high contrast, shadows, and optimum abdominal shading. After that, just sit back on a decline bench-press and wait for the LIKES to come pouring in. See how much better you feel about not booking that job? You could use social media to share interesting news with your friends, or let people know when your show is papering tickets – but wouldn't they be much more satisfied with a pair of free house seats to your abs?

5.
FIND A WAY TO RELATE TO EVERYTHING

A big part of social media is about engaging with your friends and fans. That is why it is always cool to LIKE a friend's post and then comment below about how it pertains to your life. For example, when one of my friends posted about how they loved Kristin Chenoweth on her latest canceled television series, I immediately LIKED it, and then talked about how sweet Kristin is in real life. It really helps to relate to your friends!

There will come a time when you don't necessarily book every job for which you audition. That is totally OK. Find a way to spin it into something positive. Like, one time I sat down in front of the TV for a sensible veg-fest, and saw someone performing a guest spot that should have been mine. If this happens to you,

I suggest taking to Twitter with a good old fashioned, *Remember That Time?* :

Remember that time I just wanted to watch thirty minutes of TV and all that was on was the episode of that guest star I didn't book?

You can then throw in a fun hashtag, such as #grumpy or #actorproblems. This will assure your friends that you frequently audition for TV and film, are too busy to watch more than thirty minutes of it, and found a way to successfully usurp the power that was taken from you when you did not book a job. The added bonus is that all your friends will think you're self-deprecating!

6.
<u>MAKE A FACEBOOK FAN PAGE</u>

Did you recently get new headshots? Are you performing in Upstate New York this summer? Do you have roughly 239 Twitter followers that consist of your friends, coworkers, and people with an egg icon? Then you, my friend, are ready to create your very own Facebook Fan Page!

It's not enough for people to just be your friends on Facebook. They must also be your fans. Remember: friends are fans in disguise – and your fans are going to love getting a chance to see a side of you that Twitter doesn't really present to them. I mean, 140 characters is simply not enough space in a bio to share how #blessed you are. A fan page gives you the opportunity to really let loose with your self-promotion. Go crazy! Dig up old show programs, photos, reviews, your updated résumé, and make sure to projectile vomit that shit right onto the World Wide Web.

Once you have created your fan page, you should start gathering LIKES. You can do this by personally inviting all of your Facebook friends. They'll love you for it! The most glorious words in the English language have to be, "[Insert Random Actor Friend from College] has invited you to LIKE [Insert Same Random Actor Friend from College]."

Don't get depressed if you do not receive a LIKE from every single one of your friends. Their loss! You may have to put in a little extra #werk. Wait a week or two and invite everyone again. However, whatever you do, please refrain from purchasing LIKES. Hiring a company to provide you with abundant robot followers is just plain sad – like an unofficial sign-up list.

7.
ASK YOUR FRIENDS FOR MONEY

Do you have an extracurricular activity you enjoy? Is your fun pet-project suddenly demanding a bit more money to finance? Are you horny for handouts? Kickstarter.com is the place for you! There's no time like the present to gather appropriate funding in order to move forward with your #sidedreams.

I know what you're thinking, "I have some cash saved up from this weekly Production Contract salary. I could probably spare $4,000 to fund my own debut album." LOL. Wrong! The only way to get your project funded is by jonesing up your friends for their lunch money in exchange for a Facebook SHOUT OUT!

Your closest friends will be the most sympathetic to your goal, and therefore the last people to feel alienated when you continuously bombard them with requests. True friends don't give a shit. If you have an alumni page on Facebook, you should repetitively post links to your crowdfunding website there, too. You'll get more traffic if you're one of the few successful graduates from your school, because you'll be an inspiration to those still pounding the pavement. You can even go as far as to call people out for not donating on your newly minted Facebook Fan Page. Say something like, "I've noticed that some of my friends haven't donated yet. It's not about me. It's about the art!" That should work.

Also, make certain to provide amazing perks for all your friends who contribute. The more focused the rewards are on you, the better. Putting a price tag on yourself is going to make you appear much more valuable. You're going to reach your fundraising goal a lot faster offering questionably useful shit to your friends that six or seven months ago they probably could have gotten from you for free.

Finally, when raising money under a Kickstarter deadline, it's important to seriously not give a shit. Throw caution and credibility to the curb. Ignore the fact that when your project recoups its investment, your backers will not be reimbursed. Try to forget that after requesting donations from friends, it will only be a few short months before you ask them all to buy that thing. #whatever. All is fair in love, war, and fanatically crowdfunded fantasies.

8.
DEALING WITH SOCIAL MEDIA OFFENDERS

I am #grateful to have so many Facebook friends #werking in show business. In fact, I think it's safe to say that 96% of my online social circle consists of actors, musicians, writers, etc. The other 4% belong to stage door creepers and my mom – but they are obviously all on "limited profile." It recently came to my attention that surrounding myself with such a niche group of people might be providing me with a rather tunnel-vision view of what it's like to function as an adult in society.

I used to have a lot of Facebook friends from high school who grew up to be things like doctors, lawyers, and business executives, but the moment one of them changed their last name or Instagrammed a baby, I was like, "Stop making me feel old!" #unfriend. So, I guess I don't really know a lot about people who went to college to receive a BS FBO (Bachelor of Something to Fall Back On) or how they behave on social media. How cool would it be if non-theatrical folk were just like us?

Doctors

Removing a brain tumor this afternoon. Positive vibes at 4pm!!!

Remember that time I saved two kids' lives in one workday? #SoBlessedToBeABlessing

Oh, you know… Just took the saphenous vein from the leg and attached it around the blockage in my patient's coronary artery to provide perfusion to the heart muscle. #NoBigDeal

Lawyers

Just got my client off death row. The Secret really does work!

Big news regarding a case! Wish I could share!

First day of school representing a double homicide! #werk

Business Executives

Only been with the firm six months and already two promotions! #MakingItHappen

All of my investment strategies achieved a positive return this month. When it rains, it pours! #HedgeFundRealness

Gym, eight-hour werkday, grocery shopping, home cooked dinner! #2013isNAILINGIT

Alas, this is not really the case. Instead, we have to hear them gush about their loving families, stay aloof about their jobs that pay more than $1,807 a week, and talk about having Saturdays off. That kind of passive aggressive bragging is exactly why it's important to occasionally make a few cuts within your social media circle. However, before you #unfriend someone, I suggest you leave the following citation on their wall:

VIOLATION

WE REGRET TO INFORM YOU THAT THIS FRIENDSHIP IS NO
LONGER VALID DUE TO VIOLATIONS OF APPROPRIATE INTERNET
BEHAVIOR AND/OR HUMAN DECENCY STANDARDS.

ONE OR MORE OF THE FOLLOWING ITEMS ARE IN VIOLATION:

1. Promotes conduct lacking in tact and/or self control

2. Adversely affects the efficient progress of common sense

3. Defies the very meaning of being self aware

4. Creates potential damage to electronics from the need to throw across the room

5. Blatant representation of a critical need for attention

UNFRIEND

IN CONCLUSION: BE AWARE OF YOUR UNAWARENESS

This could come as a complete shock, but some of your friends might not appreciate how you behave on social media. They may hide you on their newsfeed, unfriend you, or just plain hate-watch you. Some of them might even go as far as to take screen captures of everything you post and share them privately with their close friends via one epic group text. That is why the single most important advice I can give you about how to Social Netwerk is this: Be aware of your projected unawareness. Live your Internet *your way* and don't give a shit – as long as you're conscious of how your online behavior will be perceived by others. You're playing the game and the game has changed. Your persona on social media is just as important as the one you present in the audition room, invited dress rehearsal, or casting associate's birthday party. Make each Social Netwerking action a calculated one.

You may burn a few bridges with random acquaintances along the way, but your real friends should understand. Whether your Social Netwerking footprint evokes annoyance or accolades, at least you're making people feel something – which is more than I can say for those who choose to be boring. The entire purpose of modern art is to make the viewer feel something. Consider yourself a modern art piece! Be it a rope coming out of a wall, Tilda Swinton in a glass case, or a gigantic pile of trash lying in the corner of the MoMa, modern art can induce confusion, disillusion, and even disgust. So, go forth unto cyberland, my actor friends, and be one, big, gigantic pile of trash.

8 CURTAIN CALL

Tonight was truly magical. So many people were part of it. I wept through curtain call. #blessed #livingthedream #theatrelove

*

AND – Scene. There is nothing more I can teach you about how to #werk in show business – unless the sales of this book merit a trilogy. If that is the case, I'm ready to pump out *#GRATEFUL: Thank you, Telsey* and *#BOOKEDIT: Acting Techniques That Will Make You Werk*, because I'll do anything for a dollar. Until that time, we must accept the fact that all good things come to an end. We have reached the final curtain. Feel free to read this chapter while listening to Coldplay's "Fix You."

We'll always have the memories. It seems like only yesterday we were sifting through college acceptance letters. Now look at you – you're out there taking jobs away from me. I couldn't be more proud. I'll always cherish this time we spent together. As you continue to progress in your career and quest to bring new meaning to what it is to be #blessed, I ask that you don't forget me. I'll always be there. I am just behind the curtain, snapping my fingers up high in the air, exclaiming "WERK!" I am on the Bares poster or swinging a Mark Fisher Fitness kettlebell. I am in front of you in the Schmackary's line and behind you at that gypsy run. I am blocking the mirror at a dance audition. I am nailing a callback right before it's your turn to go into the room. My vocal warm-ups will forever emanate down the halls at every studio with subtle annoyance. I'll be practicing my sides out loud in World Wide Plaza or asking you who your agent is because mine doesn't do TV and film. I am in the dressing room selfie, the Kickstarter, and the first day of school. Whenever someone Instagrams a script – I'll be there. Whenever someone posts a motivational quote – I'll be there. Whenever someone is younger than you – I'll be there. I'll be in the hashtags – forever.

As I take my bow, I can only hope that the front row of rush seats leap to their feet, causing a default standing ovation from the remainder of the audience. Thank you – I am #grateful. You began this journey knowing you were #blessed, but now I think it is safe to say that you're officially… #SOBLESSED.

9 A BACKSTAGE TOUR

*

Thank you for purchasing #*SOBLESSED: the Annoying Actor Friend's Guide to Werking in Show Business.* If you have reached this chapter, you either skipped ahead due to disinterest, or you made it through my over-bloated blog post that I lovingly refer to as *Annoying Actor Friend and the Order of the Phoenix.* Congratulations! Now that you have reached the end, I would like to take a few more minutes of the time you devoted to reading this on the subway, at tech rehearsal, or in music theory class, to give you a behind the scenes look and fairly transparent analysis of my parody Twitter account-turned-blog-turned-how-to-book, and general distraction from my real life, Annoying Actor Friend.

Before all of this began, a friend of mine said, "Twitter is where people go to feign relevance." This person did not have a Twitter account, so I assumed he did not understand it. Then I thought of my personal account's meager two hundred and forty followers – which consisted of a handful of friends, companies I had never heard of, and nameless folk with an egg avatar. If my friend's assertions were correct, then I was unabashedly irrelevant.

Who was even I talking to? Why was I doing it at all? Why does anyone tweet? I could dive into a trite philosophical discussion about the Twitterverse, but that would risk boring you to shit, when all I really want to know is – why was I writing what I thought to be profoundly funny tweets and essentially auditioning them under the false hopes that a Twitter juggernaut like Rob Delaney would retweet them, thus garnering me hundreds of followers and steam rolling my social media existence into something worthwhile? More importantly, why was I bringing my work home with me?

When actors don't get validation from good auditions, positive feedback, callbacks, or an actual booking, then we need to find a way to source that desire elsewhere. There is such a thing as over-sharing and I am not entirely sure the majority of people, myself included, really care that much. We take to social media with our frustrations and elations because we just cannot keep them on the shelf. The simple act of a "like" or "retweet" from a friend or complete stranger lets us know that someone else is out there saying, "I'm right there with you. You matter." That action fulfills our primal need for attention. Once the craving is satisfied, we transition back into society until the urge strikes again.

Let us assume that since you are reading this book, you are a well-adjusted Awaresie who does not commit social media atrocities – or at the very least, knows how to ration your social media masturbation so you don't become a serial offender. But, what happens when a friend's public addiction to validation reaches heights that eventually make them insufferable? You can block them, un-friend them, or hate-watch them. Still, even when I take joy in screen capturing an offender's post and sending it to friends who share in the hate-watching of that individual, there is a part of me that goes to a dark place of resentment. I remember a moment before I created Annoying Actor Friend when a peer from my school went through a weekend social media humble-brag bender, and after I expressed my feelings about it to a colleague, she said, "Oh, he's just really proud!" and I responded, "Great. He can call his mom." Was I just annoyed? Envious? Disillusioned? All of it? This peer was merely one of several friends who were pushing me further and further away from them by unknowingly, and unintentionally, making me feel badly about where I was in my career.

Would you go up to a homeless person and tell them that you have an apartment and how grateful you are for it? Would you tell a friend whose show just closed, how blessed you are that your show is going to Broadway in the spring? Why do we think it is acceptable to blast that behavior to over a thousand people while safely hidden behind the cold backlight of our own personal megaphone? I had made my social media mistakes in the past and was trying to learn from them while it seemed people I knew were actually getting worse. Finally, I threw my hands up and said, "I can't take this shit anymore." I wish there were a cool story about how I spent weeks developing a deeply layered Twitter persona. Nope. I was bored, it was hot, and someone I did not even know typed the "blessed" that broke this jaded camel's back.

It took roughly seven minutes to create the account. Three to deal with the limited characters allowed in the name, two to rethink the handle because my first choice was taken by someone who had not tweeted in four years, one to type the bio, "When it rains, it pours!" and one final minute to Google image search, "annoying actor," and choose the first photo that popped up… Ellis from season one of *Smash*. The uneasiness that I felt whenever Ellis appeared on screen is the exact same emotion I feel when one of my friends behaves like an "annoying actor friend." His picture was used to link a preconceived feeling with my writing. I figured if you saw a picture of Ellis and read the word "blessed," it would all sort of make sense. Annoying Actor Friend was meant to be a quality. Not a literal persona.

Now that the account was created, it was time to experiment with the content. After tweeting, "The Secret really does work," "I am so blessed," and a few examples of, "#ReasonsIDidntBookIt," I sent a text to a friend to ask them if they found it as funny as me. When they concurred, I did what any enthusiastic go-getter does – absolutely nothing until I was drunk. After downing one or four alcoholic beverages that night, I proceeded to follow roughly three hundred actors ranging from college theatre majors to random celebrities (most of whom I did not know personally), and retreated to my bedroom to pass out for the remainder of the evening.

Upon awakening, I was astounded to find that not only was I devoid of a hangover, I had gathered thirty followers over night. This was an unbelievable accomplishment considering my personal Twitter account had failed to attract thirty followers in the previous two years. Before I started, I thought I was the only one who found the genre of actors I was parodying to be obnoxious. This accidental social media experiment was proving I was not alone. In addition to my new audience, I received a few mentions from other users complementing my account. It was rewarding, and considering I was in the middle of a career drought, I thought, "This must be what callbacks feel like!"

The tone for the account was inconsistent at first. Occasionally I would write creative content, but I often drifted from my own tweets to tweeting at actors who said things I found annoying, to just doing straight retweets. There was risk involved, but what did I care? I was anonymous and my followers were urging me to become somewhat of a social media police. The attention was addicting. Casting directors I could never get appointments from were suddenly retweeting me. Actors and writers that I admired were now following me. I think people connected to the account because they all thought it was someone they knew. People were so convinced it was the person sitting next to them in the dressing room, that nobody ever stopped to wonder if I were a bored accountant who knows a lot of theatre people and is just really observant.

Anonymity during this process caused a few problems when I finally met certain people I had conversed with through my fake account. Sometimes they would say, "Nice to meet you," and I would stumble and say something like, "I think we've met before, but I can't remember where... Um... No, wait... Nice to meet you, too." There were also times I would recognize someone who followed me and almost wave, like when you see an obscure celebrity and think it is one of your friends, then stop and say to yourself, "Nope. You don't know them. That's Carrot Top."

After the first week, certain circumstances urged me to delete the account. I worried about how it could affect my career or that of the people close to me. However, the amounting followers were addicting. By the time I had reached one thousand, I only wanted more. As summer turned into fall, I realized I was essentially milking the same joke and if I wanted this deliberate life-distracting hobby to last much longer, I would need to evolve before the novelty wore off. [Cue movie montage to the song "Hip to Be Square" by Huey Lewis & the News looped over images of me tweeting about the *Rebecca* scandal, fall shows opening, fall shows closing, Russell Crowe as Javert, a #blessed here, and a #grateful there – as we transition to February, 2013 and the impending season two premiere of *Smash*.]

Without *Smash*, this book would not exist. Up until the point *Smash* returned for its sophomore season, I had been confined to one hundred and forty characters and had been looking for an excuse to expand. I just could not figure out what to write about. Enter, *Smash*. Since alcohol and *Smash* already went hand in hand, I figured I would write a drinking game to be played while watching the season premiere. You can imagine my surprise when I learned there were already six hundred and sixty-seven drinking games devoted to *Smash*. What I hoped would set mine apart was that it was designed to be as much about actors watching *Smash* as it was about *Smash*. For example: Drink whenever someone complains about *Smash* not being realistic. Drink whenever someone at your party name-drops a friend on *Smash*. Drink whenever you get so upset at *Smash* that it becomes necessary to exit the room.

The week I posted, "Get SMASHed," I received a tweet from a follower requesting that an Annoying Actor Friend blog become a fully realized thing. At that point I was working off a free Tumblr, which I actually had no idea how to operate, and at the mere suggestion from *one* person to expand the blog, I was like, "You like me?! Sure! I'll make it a thing! Anything for attention!" So, I desperately threw down twelve dollars for a domain name and a little bit more to self-host the site. Let it be noted, I did it fully knowing I would never make a dime off of annoyingactorfriend.com. I did it because a small amount of people enjoyed my work and wanted to read more.

With *Smash*'s return, I found that I could write a weekly recap of the show that incorporated facets of the business I wanted to lampoon, while at the same time spoofing how most of our community got unusually high off of complaining about *Smash* – and I could also make fun of *Smash*. It was also an exciting excuse to make a meme of Bernard Telsey next to Gene Wilder as Willy Wonka. A win-win!

Borrowing from the viral YouTube sensation, "The Crazy Nastyass Honey Badger," I aptly titled my *Smash* recaps, "SMASH Don't Give a Shit!" and equated the series to a primarily African indigenous carnivorous weasel that is able to hunt and feed on venomous cobras because it just does not give a shit. There was always something about *Smash* that got under people's skin. Like it was actively trying to piss us off. My premise that *Smash* did not give a shit about being realistic to Broadway, and that I loved them for it, became the framing device for my weekly recaps. Finally, I had a platform to write about theatre, under the guise of making fun of annoying actors who complain about *Smash*, while literally complaining about *Smash*. The concept's intentional but exceedingly labored internal layering was over thought, and not something I am convinced ever truly came across. What did I care? As far as I was concerned, nobody was going to read it anyway. I didn't give a shit!

The fact is, my first few recaps pretty much fell on deaf ears. Then came episode three, "The Dramaturg." That was the episode when the production team for *Bombshell*, the fictitious musical within the series, hired a "show doctor" to help with the libretto – except they called him a "dramaturg." You can imagine the horror that ensued within my circle of friends by that inaccuracy. Naturally, I had a blast writing the recap, and when I posted it the following evening, I expected nothing. When I woke the next day, "SMASH Don't Give a Shit!" had found its way to Facebook and I had messages from cast members of the show. Uh-oh.

I will always stand by the professionalism of everyone involved with making *Smash*. Broadway shows get panned and picked apart all the time, but not to the extreme that was done to *Smash*. Broadway-hate is fairly local and usually among friends. *Smash*-hate was national and public. It appeared that since it was a television show, it was fair game to gripe about freely on Facebook. It was like people forgot that they might be friends with a cast member. When it is a Broadway show someone is disenchanted with, there is a rare chance they criticize it publicly. Facebook is questionable with its constant profile privacy changes, and any comment you make may randomly end up on a creative team member's newsfeed. *Smash* was another world's interpretation of our world, and therefore something close enough for us to care a great deal about, but far enough away that it seemed making fun of it would not necessarily harm us professionally.

My response from people on the show was mostly positive. Some cast members complimented me on the recaps and some thought I was Wesley Taylor. I am not Wesley Taylor. I promise you Wesley Taylor has much more productive things to do with his time. There were also people involved with the show that I knew personally, and I think they may have been thrown by my very public and critical analysis. This was difficult for me to explain because I was freely able to say whatever I wanted to while hiding behind a persona. I tried to play it off like I was writing some meta essay commenting on the general stiff-handing of *Smash* by the industry, and not the show itself – but who was I kidding? I guarantee nobody read it for what I was masquerading it as. There were plenty of recaps out there and I believe mine was the only one that tried to get more "insiderey" than *Smash* itself. *Smash* may have had references to Jennifer Damiano and Jessie Mueller, but I made jokes about Corey Cott never having to ever attend an EPA. There was a niche audience I had attracted and once again, I fell victim to the attention.

It was not until after my fourth recap of *Smash* that a reader chastised me for not being Rachel Shukert at *The Vulture*, and that I should cease writing immediately. Having never heard of Rachel Shukert, I decided to look into her *Smash* recaps to see for myself. After reading a recap where Ms. Shukert artfully equated the character of Karen Cartwright to the human equivalent of something far more obscure and witty than anything I had ever written, it registered what all the talk was about. Point being, had I known about Rachel Shukert's recaps, I never would have started writing my own. I realize that is like saying, "Had I known people could sing higher, dance better, and act stronger than me, I never would have pursued musical theatre in the first place."

The most thrilling part of the process came when cast members and writers of *Smash* shared my recaps, but nothing was more mind-blowing than a rumor that one of Steven Spielberg's assistants *might* be a reader. Upon hearing this, I desperately tried to get Mr. Spielberg's attention by drafting a public letter to the famous director, suggesting how he could help boost *Smash*'s ratings by incorporating elements from his films into the series. I spent three days with a free online movie font generator and the screen capture function, archaically reconstructing classic artwork by shoehorning *Smash* references into film posters of *Jaws, Indian Jones, Schindler's List,* and others. Of all the content I ever published about *Smash*, the blog dedicated to Steven Spielberg was my proudest moment. Come on – *Indiana Jones and the Second Hand White Baby Grand?* I thought that was genius. It bombed. No matter how many times I tweeted the link, I could not generate traffic for that blog post. I guess the audience for supernatural Broadway themed action films is limited. The first scene in *Indian Jones and the Temple of Doom* is of the Rockettes kicking to "Anything Goes," sung almost completely in Mandarin. That actually happened. How could a representation of the *Schindler's List* poster re-imagined as *Hit List* be so off target and underappreciated? It goes to show that even when you think you have written the smartest, wittiest content, or found the sixteen bars that show you off best, or know in your heart that you are exactly the type they are looking for, you just might be wrong. You just might not be what the people behind the table see when they close their eyes.

Then *Smash* ended. Megan Hilty and Rachel Shukert moved to Los Angeles. Jeremy Jordan did a movie. Krysta Rodriguez went back to Broadway. Katharine McPhee made an album. Everyone else moved on and I was left alone in my quest to feign relevance. I needed a new prospect. That was when I got inspired to take my "SMASH Don't Give a Shit!" writing style and apply it to this analysis of what life is like for aspiring actors and actresses in today's world. In lieu of trying to find a publisher, literary agent, and anything else a serious writer might do, I poured over my computer for about three months, gave it a brief once-over with a friend or two, and uploaded it myself onto Amazon. As far as I was concerned, I had spent enough time pounding the pavement in real life, I certainly was not going to do the same when it came to my after school activity.

Looking back on this experience, I cannot help but acknowledge how it affected me. It began as a stupid joke. I was frustrated with my friends, of course, but none of what I was doing ever stemmed from malice. If I were lucky, perhaps it would spread a little awareness. Maybe I could stop one college kid, professional actor, friend, or myself from making someone feel worse about his or her own status quo – or at least from projectile vomiting their Cheerios across the room. Once people started to agree with me, the entire accidental experiment progressed into a means for attention.

Ironically, the very tool I was using to poke fun

at attention-starved behavior on social media was providing me with a platform to attract the positive recognition I did not realize I needed myself. It went from being a silly distraction to a serious obsession. Should I tweet that? How can I turn this current event into a theatre-related joke? How many followers did I get today? Did I have a solid amount of retweets this week? Refresh the mentions. Tweet something. Wait. Refresh the mentions. Repeat – I became exactly what I was satirizing.

Perhaps, during my trendy gravitation toward the bitter and jaded cynical side of the psyche that is too often encouraged in this business, I forgot what it was like to be fucking super excited about something. The only thing that stopped me from posting on my Facebook about how cool I thought it was that Rob Delaney favorited one of my tweets or that I was being followed by multiple verified accounts, was the fact that saying anything would have blown my cover. Having that crucial filter taught me that while I was ecstatic about those random accomplishments, who really gave a shit about my parody Twitter account? In a very short time, I went from hating annoying actors, to empathizing with them, to becoming them, to ultimately learning that restraint is possible, and that participating in annoying actor friend behavior is not something I'll ever do – but I understand it.

My time playing Bruce Wayne to Annoying Actor Friend has taught me that tact and appropriate social media behavior is sometimes a grey area. I have friends who need their successes noted and those who do not. I have found that I fall somewhere in the middle. Perhaps the best option for us is to understand what we need as an artist and find a way to get it without being offensive, or learn that we do not "need" it as much as we thought we did. If we can all find a way to be socially aware while walking the line of obnoxiousness, maybe our little world will be a slightly less douchey place.

10 @ACTOR_FRIEND: A RETROSPECTIVE

A categorized look back at tweets from Annoying Actor Friend's first year.

#Blessed...

if you say "#blessed" in the mirror three times a non-equity kid will appear & tell you he's getting his card with his Broadway debut.

Somewhere in my youth or childhood, I must have done something good. #SoBlessed

I feel like I'm drowning in a sea of audition material, but the truth is I'm drowning in a sea of blessings!

Every time #Blessed trends on Twitter, some kid books a Broadway show right out of college.

I need to start counting blessings instead of sheep. #insomnia

I'm soy blessed I became vegan.

I've had #blesseder days.

Bonjour! Je suis béni. #BastilleBlessed

I crapped rose petals this morning. #bowelblessed

It took me nine months but I finally got death threats! I feel #SoBlessed. It really goes to show what happens when you put in the #werk.

Current Topics & Events...

I haven't been tweeting much lately because I'm working on my craft. And by, "working on my craft," I mean watching Orange is the New Black.

Orange is the New Callback.

Johnny Depp as Tonto brings new meaning to the phrase, "All ethnicities are encouraged to attend."

$5 to the first SAG actor to change their name to North West so that kid has to use her middle initial when she gets her own reality show.

Happy Father's Day! Here's to the guy who was supportive when I was like, "I'm not into sports, but I hear Annie is in town!" #thanksdad

That final "Game of Thrones" scene was a fairly honest metaphor for a chorus call when you're over 30. #cutthroat #notblessed

Whoever scheduled the Tonys on the same night as the Game of Thrones finale is one sick fuck.

NBC took a bigger dump on Broadway this week than the impostor Cookie Monster I saw squatting in the corner of the 50th St 1 train platform.

With all the countries passing Marriage Equality, it feels like "So Long, Fare Well" and America is dumb ass Gretl passed out on the steps.

Why did I accept his friend request? I don't know. We had 47 red equal signs in common...

As that one girl in HAIR once said, "As Mary Magdalene once said, 'Jesus, I'm getting stoned!' " #happy420

Seeing what Grumpy Cat has achieved by her first birthday gives me the same feeling as when I see "Class of '12" in a Playbill bio.

I wonder if Anne Frank would have been a Fansie... Probably a Renthead. Definitely not a Jekkie.

I live every day like it's Good Friday... always #nailingit.

Happy Easter! Do you know where I can find an egg-white coloring kit?

Am I in charge of bringing the ball gags to Sondheim's sex dungeon tonight? I don't want to ruin his birthday. AGAIN.

It's St. Patrick's Day, so I'll be giving you "Erin go Braghdway" at today's matinée.

Choosing the new Pope better not be as arduous as that Karen or Ivy as Marilyn bullshit.

I think we should select the new Pope like that GREASE reality TV show. But I'd be torn between Ballerina Pope and Bellhop Pope.

NEWSFLASH: Amanda Seyfried 'eyes role' in Wicked film and my eyes 'actually' roll.

The Broadway production of ORPHANS is replacing the kid from Even Stevens with the kid from Flash Forward. #ThatsSoRaven

I was going to give up social media for Lent, but then where would I post daily status updates about what I gave up for Lent?

Don't fault the 49ers for their terrible game play. I don't think any man from San Fran can breathe after Beyonce's halftime performance.